beautiful *food*

beautiful *food*

Healthy recipes to nourish you, inside and out

JODY VASSALLO

HARLEQUIN® MIRA®

CONTENTS

HOW TO USE THIS BOOK

There are a couple of ways you can use this book. You can use it as a simple guide to healthy seasonal eating or alternatively, you can use it as an Ayurvedic cookbook.

If you choose to use it based on the seasons, then 'Foods that cool' are best cooked in summer and the hotter months, 'Foods that ground' will really benefit you on the windy days typical in spring and autumn, and 'Foods that warm' are perfect for cold wintery times.

Should you choose to use this as an Ayurvedic cookbook, I suggest you begin by looking at the chart on page 206 to determine your 'dosha', or constitution. Once you have done that, you may want to follow the menu planners on page 209 to get started and to see if you are on the right track.

- 'Foods that cool' are best for Pitta types, but can be used by most people in summer.

- 'Foods that ground' are best for Vata types, but this food can be of benefit to us all in times of stress, change and travel.

- 'Foods that warm' are best suited to Vata and Kapha types.

Most importantly, this book is about learning how to listen to your body and discovering which foods work for you. The last thing I want you to do is get finicky about getting it right – that will only create more stress! If you find the Ayurvedic approach appealing, then give it a go but try not to let it take over your life. Ayurveda is all about learning to align with nature and letting go of our desire to control things. Easier said than done, I know. But go gently, this is your life and this book is simply a tool that will hopefully help you understand how to live a healthier, happier, more balanced life.

You may not be familiar with some of the ingredients in this book. You will find many of them listed in the glossary, with a brief description of how to use them. I encourage you to venture out of your comfort zone and experiment with new tastes and flavours. This is an entirely gluten-free book so I have used some grains and flours that you may not have tasted before, but most can be found in a health food store.

So off you go and have fun. Each morning, check outside and see what the weather is doing, then take a moment to notice how you are feeling. Ask yourself, 'How can I support myself today with food so that I get the best out of my day?' Then into the kitchen you go to make yourself and those you love a nourishing breakfast; it doesn't have to be flash. I have included quite a few recipes that are suitable for cooking ahead and eating throughout the week because I hear so often how tired people are of cooking three meals a day, every day.

I encourage you to use your kitchen as your own little laboratory. If you have kids, I think it is really important for you to encourage them to cook with you. I am yet to meet a kid who doesn't like to cook. I believe our path to wellness will come through learning to appreciate the joy of being in a kitchen and cooking simple, healthy meals. Try to give each meal the time and love it deserves. Sit down together and allow yourselves to be nourished. It is that simple.

INTRODUCTION

When diet is wrong, medicine is of no use. When diet is correct, medicine is of no need. Ayurvedic proverb

Beautiful Food is about you getting to know yourself. It is about learning small, effective ways of including foods that will work for you in your diet. It is about coming to understand how you feel after you have eaten, and, without becoming obsessed, adjusting your eating habits accordingly.

I wrote this book because I want people to change their approach to food. I don't want you to eat something *just* because it is healthy; I want you to eat it because you enjoy it, you feel nourished by it and because, after eating it, you feel better for having done so. This, in my mind, is the foundation of living a healthy life. I do not believe someone is healthy just because they don't eat sugar, they only eat organic and they never eat anything considered bad for them. I do believe rigid approaches to food are not good for us or for those around us, nor are they good for children, who see us making enemies out of our food.

The food we put into our bodies can really affect our day-to-day lives. Science has finally acknowledged this with the discovery that we have what is termed a 'second brain' in our digestive system. Within our gut we have a complex nervous system that oversees the function of the whole digestive process. Seventy per cent of our immune system is focused on fighting off possible invaders, like viruses and bacteria, and maintaining a delicate balance. And we now know that the state of our digestive health is important for our wellbeing. Up to 90 per cent of the neurotransmitter serotonin is produced in the gut. We need serotonin to feel happy, but if our gut is not functioning the way it should, we will find it really hard to see the good stuff life has to offer. The enteric nervous system in the gut is also very sensitive to emotional and psychological stresses. I recommend you pay special attention to the foods you eat at stressful times. Ask anyone with a digestive complaint and they will tell you their condition is always worse when they are stressed or tired.

True health comes from having a healthy, relaxed outlook on life. It comes from having loving relationships, a happy home, regular exercise, faith, money and gratitude. It comes from dealing with stress and avoiding eating food that won't support you in times of stress. Food is only a small part of what makes us healthy. And I honestly can't see why everyone takes it so seriously. We are fortunate to have it in plentiful supply and of such great quality, and I think it is about time we began to celebrate the beauty it can bring to our lives and be grateful for that.

I believe that there is no single diet that suits everyone. Instead, I believe we are individuals with individual needs. We have different body shapes, different hopes, dreams and desires, and most definitely different nutritional requirements. I have spent many years researching these beliefs and found that the Ayurvedic system, developed 5000 years ago in India, had figured this out centuries ago.

About 10 years ago now, I started playing around with the idea of looking at the world, people and food from an Ayurvedic standpoint. I discovered that people could be roughly divided into three different body types or doshas – Vata, Pitta or Kapha – and then, through looking into the eating recommendations for these different body types, I was able to establish foods that were suitable for me to eat. I found that some of the foods I absolutely loved were my medicine and that my health improved when I regularly included them in my life. I also found, much to my disappointment, that some of the foods I loved were not so good for me – kind of like a bad relationship, but we won't go into that!

So, it was through a relaxed, honest and moderate approach to my health, and ultimately my happiness, that I established a collection of recipes: foods I could eat in summer that would cool me down, physically and mentally; foods I could turn to when I was feeling wobbly, when I had been travelling too much and needed to be grounded and nurtured; and foods I could bunker down with in winter that would provide the energy to function in the world.

And I came to understand that taste is a really important sense – what I feel like and what I need on certain days may differ greatly. I learnt that sugar will never make you truly feel better long term, but it doesn't mean you can't enjoy it on occasion, in moderation and not feel guilty about it. In Ayurveda, sweet is used to cool and ground, and is not considered the enemy, but it is also not meant to be eaten every day or at the end of every meal. I learnt that cold uncooked foods don't sit well with me outside the hotter months. I learnt that my needs changed with the seasons, as does the food Mother Nature provides.

I could go on and on about what I learnt but that is not the point of this introduction. I want to encourage you to learn what is right for you and to share your insight with your friends. Don't try to prescribe to them what you think they should be eating, that will just make them cross – trust me, I've tried it. Instead, share your experiences and talk only of how this approach to food has worked for you. People will see for themselves how happy and healthy you are. And please, please, please don't give yourself a hard time if you don't do it perfectly.

That brings me to the 90/10 rule I live by. I eat the good stuff 90 per cent of the time, then allow myself the other not-so-great stuff 10 per cent of the time. I find this helps me avoid a big blow out when my rebellious streak comes out to play. I don't ever try to give something up, instead I just aim to crowd it out with other, more beneficial, foods. If sugar has crept back into my diet, I don't tell myself I am not having any, which usually just makes me want it even more, I try to eat loads of fruits and vegetables.

If it all sounds a little too simple, that's because it is. This is your life, your body, and you are free to choose what you put into it. Hopefully, the recipes within these pages will provide you with the inspiration to make healthy, informed choices every day. The recipes are simple; believe me, I am a no-fuss cook. I don't peel stuff and I don't like to fluff around in the kitchen making my food look like it has been produced in a restaurant. I don't plate up for people – I have no idea how much anyone wants or needs to eat, so I always let them serve themselves. And as much as I love to socialise, I try to give my food the love and attention it deserves when I eat. I am learning to put my fork and knife down between bites and not hurry the process. This way my brain has time to register I am eating and my body can tell me when I am feeling full.

I know that no one can ever eat too many vegetables and that Mother Nature provides us with all we need to be truly happy beings. It is just up to us to get a little more in tune with ourselves so we can fully appreciate that.

Enjoy your journey and remember: if your body is reacting to a food you've eaten, then it is trying to tell you something. Listening to your body is one of the greatest gifts you can give yourself. I invite you to turn down the volume of your mind and drop down into your belly, the source of much wisdom and knowledge.

There is a voice that doesn't use words. Listen. ~ Rumi

FOODS THAT COOL
for hot days

APPLES, ASPARAGUS, AVOCADO, BANANAS, BASMATI RICE, BERRIES, BROCCOLI, CAULIFLOWER, CELERY, CHICKPEAS, COCONUT, CORIANDER, COW'S MILK, CUCUMBER, CURRY LEAVES, DATES, DILL , ELDERFLOWER, FENNEL, FIGS, GHEE , GOAT'S MILK, GREEN BEANS, GREEN MANGO, JASMINE RICE, KALE, LAVENDER, LEMONGRASS, LEMONS, LETTUCE, LIMA BEANS, LIMES, MAPLE SYRUP, MELON, MINT, MUNG BEANS, PEARS, PEAS, PINTO BEANS, POMEGRANATE, PRUNES, QUINCE, RAISINS, RHUBARB, ROCKET, ROSE, SAFFRON, SPLIT PEAS, SPROUTS, STRAWBERRIES, SUNFLOWER SEEDS, TAMARIND, TOFU, TURMERIC, VANILLA, WATERMELON, WITLOF, ZUCCHINI, APPLES, ASPARAGUS...

breakfast

Baked ricotta with smoky beans, asparagus and kale

Baked ricotta makes a perfect summer breakfast and the crisp kale chips are a great accompaniment to the smooth, creamy ricotta. If you want to serve this dish in winter, sprinkle the ricotta with some warming spices and add a can of chopped tomatoes to the beans.

Preheat the oven to 200°C. Line two baking trays with baking paper.

Place the ricotta on one of the trays and drizzle on half the oil. (Avoid seasoning with salt and pepper as these are heating.) Bake for 20 minutes, until golden. Set aside and keep warm.

Place the asparagus and kale on the second tray and brush lightly with half of the remaining oil. Bake for 10 minutes, until the kale is crisp and the asparagus is tender.

Heat the rest of the oil in a frying pan over medium heat, add the fennel seeds and paprika and cook for 1 minute, until fragrant. Add the lima beans and cook for 10 minutes, until heated through.

Serve the baked ricotta with the asparagus, kale and smoky beans.

Serves 6–8

1 kg wheel full-fat ricotta
1 tablespoon olive oil, plus extra to drizzle
12 asparagus spears, woody ends trimmed
200 g kale leaves, stems removed
1 teaspoon fennel seeds
1 teaspoon sweet smoked paprika
2 x 400 g cans lima beans, rinsed and drained

Salt water is very heating, so make sure you rinse yourself off after the beach in summer.

Iced matcha and maple tea

Whisk the matcha tea powder with 125 ml (½ cup) of cold water until frothy. Gradually whisk in the milk, then sweeten with the maple syrup. Serve in small cups.

Serves 4

2 tablespoons matcha green tea powder, sifted
500 ml (2 cups) chilled unsweetened almond milk or milk of your choice
1 teaspoon pure maple syrup

Coconut, strawberry and quinoa bircher muesli

You can use rice flakes for this recipe instead of quinoa flakes if you like. Coconut yoghurt is a little pricey but it is perfect to use here as it is more cooling than other yoghurts. If you can't be bothered to grate the strawberries, then thinly slice them; however, grating them gives you lots of juice, which adds a pretty pink colour to the muesli.

Put the quinoa flakes, apple juice, yoghurt, vanilla, strawberries, pepitas and chia seeds into a large bowl and mix well to combine. Cover and refrigerate overnight.

In the morning, loosen the muesli with a little more apple juice.

To serve, spoon the muesli into bowls, top with the mixed berries and drizzle with a little maple syrup.

Serves 8

190 g (2 cups) quinoa flakes
400 ml unsweetened apple juice, plus extra to serve
260 g (1 cup) coconut yoghurt or Greek-style yoghurt
1 teaspoon natural vanilla extract
200 g strawberries, grated
2 tablespoons pepitas
1 tablespoon white chia seeds
200 g mixed berries, to serve
pure maple syrup, to drizzle

Egg white omelette with asparagus, peas and goat's feta

I have used only egg whites in this recipe, as the yolk is the fatty, heating part of the egg. Chickpeas are cooling and can often be a little hard to digest for those with sensitive tummies, which is why I use hummus instead, as the tahini warms the chickpeas and does not create so much gas.

If you have ever seen asparagus grow, you will know that for it to grow straight and tall, the earth needs to be mounded up around it. I believe the same is true for us in a sense: without a strong connection to the earth we inhabit, we will all struggle to maintain our equilibrium.

Whisk together the egg whites until soft peaks form.

Heat half the oil in a large non-stick frying pan, add half the egg white and cook over medium heat until just set.

Dot half the hummus over the top, then scatter on half the peas, feta, asparagus and mint. Cover with a lid and cook until the egg white is set.

Keep warm while you cook a second omelette with the remaining ingredients. Serve immediately.

Serves 4

8 free-range egg whites
1 tablespoon olive oil
2 tablespoons hummus
40 g (¼ cup) frozen baby peas
50 g goat's feta
6 asparagus spears, lightly blanched and halved lengthways
a small handful of mint leaves, roughly chopped

Asparagus is a tridoshic vegetable, making it suitable for all doshas. It is cooling, as well as grounding and stabilising.

The ultimate green hit

Green smoothies are the new thing in the world of health. I like to add a spoonful of spirulina or chlorophyll to mine to boost the nutrient value and give me energy. The strawberry adds sweetness and the avocado gives a touch of creaminess.

Combine the celery, strawberries, avocado, cucumber, spirulina, chia seeds, kale or spinach and coconut water in a blender and blend until smooth and creamy.

Serves 2

1 celery stalk, roughly chopped
200 g strawberries, hulled
1 small avocado, chopped
1 Lebanese cucumber
1 tablespoon spirulina
1 tablespoon chia seeds
45 g (1 cup) shredded kale or baby spinach
375 ml (1½ cups) coconut water

Blueberry, almond and chia muffins

This is officially the best muffin recipe I have ever written.

Preheat the oven to 190°C. Grease a six-hole 250 ml (1 cup) muffin tin.

Sift the flour and cinnamon into a bowl. Stir in the chia seeds, almond meal, sugar and blueberries.

Whisk the buttermilk, olive oil and egg white together in a bowl until combined.

Fold the liquid ingredients into the dry ingredients and mix until just combined. Divide the mixture among the muffin holes. Bake for 25–30 minutes, until the muffins start to come away from the side of the tin. Cool slightly, then remove the muffins from the tin and serve.

Makes 6

125 g (1 cup) gluten-free self-raising flour
1 teaspoon ground cinnamon
2 tablespoons white chia seeds
100 g (1 cup) almond meal
140 g (⅔ cup) coconut sugar
125 g blueberries
250 ml (1 cup) buttermilk
3 tablespoons olive oil
1 free-range egg white

Poached stone fruit with bay, vanilla, saffron and star anise

I grew up eating stone fruit for breakfast on my cereal or for dessert with ice cream. It is funny that these days I prefer to eat it on its own.

Every summer without fail, I buy a few trays of stone fruit and bottle them. This takes up a ridiculous amount of space in my already packed fridge, but I feel ripped off if summer ends and I am without them. The poached fruit needs to be stored in the fridge because I haven't used enough sugar to preserve them at room temperature.

Preheat the oven to 100°C. Wash two 1 litre (4 cup) glass preserving jars in hot soapy water, then rinse. Place the jars upside down on a baking tray and transfer to the oven to dry. After 10 minutes, invert and continue to heat until the jars are completely dry.

Put the stone fruit into a large saucepan, add the vanilla bean, bay leaves, saffron and star anise and cover with 4 litres (16 cups) of water. Cook over medium heat for 20 minutes, until the fruit is just soft. Stir in the sugar and cook, stirring occasionally, until the sugar dissolves. Simmer for 10 minutes, then remove the fruit and place in the sterilised jars.

Boil the cooking liquid for 20 minutes, until reduced and slightly thickened. Pour over the fruit and seal with a sterilised lid. Cool and store in the refrigerator for up to 6 weeks.

Makes 2 x 1 litre (4 cup) jars

2 kg stone fruit
1 vanilla bean, split in half lengthways
2 bay leaves
pinch of saffron threads
3 star anise
185 g (1 cup) coconut sugar

I love poached fruit stirred through bircher muesli or used as a filling for pies, or on top of creamed rice pudding.

Raspberry chia pots with maple coconut tops

Chia seeds are a relatively new superfood. I love how simple they are to use and that they set just like gelatine, are a great substitute for eggs in baking and give extra crunch to crackers. Black or white, they don't really taste too different. They are heating, so that's why I have teamed them here with cooling raspberries and coconut cream.

Use a fork to crush the raspberries. Stir in the chia seeds and mix to combine.

Divide the raspberry mixture between four 125 ml (½ cup) capacity ramekins, cover and chill for 4 hours, until just set.

To make the top, combine the coconut cream, maple syrup and chia seeds in a bowl.

Spoon the top over the raspberry mixture, cover and chill for 2 hours, until set.

Serves 4

VARIATIONS:
You can use many different pureed fruits for this recipe. I like to use berries in summer as they are cooling, as are bananas, and I find kids love them. Mangoes also work well, but I make sure I team them with some lime juice as ripe mango can be heating.

500 g frozen raspberries, thawed
2 tablespoons white chia seeds

Maple coconut top
125 ml (½ cup) coconut cream
1 teaspoon pure maple syrup
1½ tablespoons white chia seeds

Yoghurt with mango, passionfruit and chia jelly

Soak the chia seeds in the passionfruit juice and mango puree for 1 hour, until a soft gel forms.

Divide the yoghurt between four serving glasses and spoon the chia jelly over the top.

Serves 4

3 tablespoons chia seeds
125 ml (½ cup) passionfruit juice
125 ml (½ cup) mango puree
520 g (2 cups) goat's milk yoghurt

Vegan coconut, banana and chia pancakes

There is no egg in this recipe, instead I have used chia seeds to bind the mixture. Soak the chia seeds in water for 5–10 minutes, stirring a few times so they don't clump together. The seeds will become an egg-white consistency. This egg replacement can be used in cakes and muffins. One tablespoon of chia seeds soaked in 3 tablespoons of water is equal to one egg.

Soak the chia seeds in 125 ml (½ cup) water for 5–10 minutes, stirring occasionally.

Meanwhile, sift the buckwheat flour, arrowroot, coconut flour and baking powder into a bowl. Stir in the shredded coconut. Make a well in the centre.

Mix together the mashed banana, coconut oil, chia mixture and coconut water. Fold the mixture into the dry ingredients, mixing until just combined.

Heat a little extra coconut oil in a large non-stick frying pan over medium heat and add 2 tablespoons of batter per pancake. Cook for 3 minutes on each side, until golden. Transfer to a plate and keep warm in the oven while you cook the remaining pancakes.

Serve the pancakes topped with slices of the butter and a good splash of maple syrup.

Serves 4–6

2 tablespoons white chia seeds
130 g (1 cup) buckwheat flour
45 g (⅓ cup) arrowroot
50 g (⅓ cup) coconut flour
1 teaspoon gluten-free baking powder
20 g (¼ cup) shredded coconut
1 small banana (about 100 g), mashed
3 tablespoons coconut oil, plus extra for cooking
300 ml coconut water
butter, to serve
pure maple syrup, to serve

Chia passion power drink

Smoothies can be a satisfying meal replacement. I don't recommend adding ice to them, especially if you are a Vata type.

Put the passionfruit juice, chopped banana, maca powder, chia seeds, spirulina and coconut water into a blender and blend until smooth and creamy.

Serves 4

250 ml (1 cup) passionfruit juice, strained
2 bananas, chopped
1 tablespoon maca powder
1 tablespoon white chia seeds
2 teaspoons spirulina
500 ml (2 cups) coconut water

lunch

Fish tacos with cabbage slaw

The ultimate summer lunch. Try to use a fish that is in season and either farmed or not threatened.

Cut the fish into large bite-sized pieces and place in a bowl. Add the cumin, paprika, lime juice and adobo sauce and mix to combine. Cover and refrigerate while you prepare the remaining ingredients.

Bring the fish to room temperature 30 minutes before cooking.

For the garlic yoghurt, whisk together the yoghurt and garlic, then cover and chill until ready to serve.

Preheat the oven to 180°C.

Wrap the tortillas in foil and put into the oven about 15 minutes before you are ready to serve.

Heat the oil in a large frying pan over medium heat, add the fish and cook, turning once, for 5 minutes, until cooked to your liking. Drain on paper towel.

Serve bowls of the garlic yoghurt, smoky tomato salsa, avocado salsa and cabbage slaw with the fish and the warmed tortillas.

Serves 6

TIP: Use the sauce but not the chilli. I like to use Embasa chipotle chillies in adobo sauce.

750 g mackerel or salmon fillets, pin-boned and skin removed
1 teaspoon ground cumin
1 teaspoon sweet smoked paprika
juice of 1 lime
1 tablespoon chipotle chilli adobo (see Tip)
12 corn tortillas
1 tablespoon olive oil

Garlic yoghurt
130 g (½ cup) Greek-style yoghurt
1 garlic clove, peeled and crushed with a pinch of sea salt

To serve
Smoky tomato salsa (page 39)
Avocado salsa (page 39)
Cabbage slaw (page 39)

Smoky tomato salsa

Heat a large non-stick frying pan over high heat, add the tomatoes, red onion and garlic and cook until the tomato skins are blackened and split and the onion and garlic are slightly charred. Remove from the pan.

Coarsely chop the tomatoes, add to a food processor with the onion, peeled garlic, coriander root, chilli and sauce and lime juice and process until coarse – you don't want it too smooth.

Set aside to allow the flavours to develop before serving.

Serves 6

2 vine-ripened tomatoes
1 small red onion, very thinly sliced
1 garlic clove, unpeeled
1 tablespoon coriander roots, scrubbed
1 chipotle chilli and 1 tablespoon adobo sauce
1 tablespoon lime juice

Avocado salsa

Put the avocado, garlic, lime juice and coriander into a bowl, then mix to combine. Cover and chill until ready to serve.

Serves 6

2 avocados, peeled, seeded and halved
2 garlic cloves, peeled and crushed with
   a pinch of sea salt
juice of 1 lime
2 tablespoons chopped coriander leaves

Cabbage slaw

Combine the cabbage, onion, coriander and mint in a bowl and mix well.

Serves 6

225 g (3 cups) finely shredded white cabbage
1 red onion, very thinly sliced
a handful of coriander leaves
a handful of mint leaves

Chopped salad with herbed chicken

If you haven't tasted a chopped salad before, you are in for a treat. The idea is to serve the salad on the chopping board, so make sure you have a really big board and try not to make too much of a mess chopping.

Put the chicken and lime slices in a large frying pan, cover with water, bring to the boil, then reduce the heat to low and poach for 25 minutes, until the chicken is cooked through. Remove from the pan and set aside to cool. Shred the chicken.

On a large chopping board, chop the spring onions. Add the cucumber and chop into the spring onion, then place the tomatoes on top and chop. Next, chop in the alfalfa sprouts, avocado, cos lettuce, herbs and chicken.

Make a well in the centre of the salad and add the mustard, verjuice and olive oil, then chop and fold into the salad.

Serves 4

2 free-range chicken breast fillets
1 lime, sliced
2 spring onions, ends trimmed
1 Lebanese cucumber, ends trimmed
100 g cherry tomatoes
a handful of alfalfa sprouts
1 avocado, peeled and halved
1 baby cos lettuce, leaves separated
a handful of mint leaves
a handful of coriander leaves
1 teaspoon dijon mustard
1 tablespoon verjuice
2 tablespoons extra virgin olive oil

In summer I live on chopped salads. They always have sprouts, cooling herbs and an avocado. I change the dressings to suit the other vegetables I add.

Fig, rocket and mozzarella salad with sticky pecans

Arrange the figs, mozzarella, pomegranate seeds and salad leaves on serving plates.

Put the eggs in a saucepan and cover with cold water. Bring to the boil, cover with a lid and turn off the heat. Leave the eggs to cook in the water for about 5 minutes, until soft boiled. Peel, cut in half and place on the salad.

To make the sticky pecans, combine the sugar and 2 tablespoons of water in a small saucepan over low heat and cook, stirring, until the sugar dissolves. Bring to the boil and cook until the syrup has reduced and thickened slightly. Add the pecans and toss to coat in the syrup. Spread the nuts out on a baking tray lined with baking paper and set aside to cool slightly. Sprinkle over the salad.

Whisk together the dressing ingredients and drizzle over the salad.

Serves 4–6

8 figs, torn into quarters
300 g buffalo mozzarella, roughly torn
3 tablespoons pomegranate seeds
200 g mixed salad leaves
8 free-range eggs

Sticky pecans
2 tablespoons coconut sugar
50 g pecans

Dressing
1 tablespoon white balsamic vinegar
1 teaspoon dijon mustard
1 teaspoon pure maple syrup
3 tablespoons extra virgin olive oil

Prawn rice paper rolls with tamarind sauce

Put the vermicelli into a heatproof bowl, cover with boiling water and allow to stand for 10 minutes, until the noodles are soft. Drain well and cut into shorter lengths.

Working with one sheet at a time, immerse the rice paper in a shallow bowl of lukewarm water until just soft.

Lay the soaked rice paper on a clean tea towel on a chopping board, top with 2 mint leaves, 2 prawn halves, 2 pieces of tofu, 1 heaped tablespoon of vermicelli, a few pieces of cucumber and some carrot and lettuce, then fold in the sides and roll up. Cover and keep moist with a piece of damp paper towel while you make the remaining rolls.

To make the dipping sauce, combine the lime juice, tamarind puree, palm sugar and 2 tablespoons of warm water in a small bowl and whisk together until the sugar dissolves.

Place rice paper rolls on a platter and serve with dipping sauce.

Makes 12

50 g rice or mung bean vermicelli
15 sheets of rice paper
24 mint leaves
12 cooked prawns, peeled, deveined and halved
150 g smoked firm tofu, cut into thin strips
1 Lebanese cucumber, cut into thin strips
1 small carrot, grated
50 g baby cos lettuce, finely shredded

Dipping sauce
3 tablespoons lime juice
1 tablespoon tamarind puree
1 tablespoon grated palm sugar

Minted coconut and chicken larb with crisp witlof

Toast the sticky rice in a dry non-stick frying pan until fragrant. Pound in a mortar and pestle until finely ground.

Put the chicken into a bowl and mash to break up.

Heat the stock in a saucepan over medium heat, add the chicken and cook for 10 minutes, until heated through. Remove and allow to cool slightly.

Add the spring onion, coconut, mint, coriander, toasted rice, lime juice, fish sauce, coconut sugar and fried shallots to the chicken and mix to combine.

Spoon the chicken larb into the witlof leaves and serve with the pickled vegetables.

Serves 4

2 tablespoons sticky rice
500 g organic chicken mince
250 ml (1 cup) chicken stock
4 spring onions, thinly sliced
4 tablespoons shredded coconut, toasted
2 handfuls of mint leaves, chopped
a handful of coriander leaves, chopped
2 tablespoons lime juice
2 tablespoons fish sauce
2 tablespoons coconut sugar
2 tablespoons fried shallots
2 witlof, leaves separated
Pickled vegetables (page 164), to serve

Fresh young coconut water is an amazing source of energy. I crack open a fresh organic coconut every morning in summer and drink the water. If I am hungry, I eat the flesh; if not, I scoop it out and freeze it for smoothies or salads. Coconut water is perfect for balancing the body's electrolytes, which allow us to feel hydrated. I don't buy bottled coconut water, as it has sugar added.

Poached lemongrass tofu and coconut lime rice

Tofu is naturally cooling and this recipe is great for a quick summer lunch. I like to bake the tofu in the oven, but if you are short on time, you can poach it in a frying pan on the stovetop. You will need a fairly firm tofu for this recipe.

Preheat the oven to 200°C.

Slice the tofu and place in a baking dish with the lemongrass, lime leaves and dashi stock. Bake for 40 minutes, until the tofu is coloured and half the liquid has been absorbed.

Add the snow peas and bok choy to the dish and return to the oven for 5 minutes, until they are bright green and tender.

Meanwhile, put the rice into a saucepan with the coconut milk and 250 ml (1 cup) of water. Bring to the boil over high heat and then cook for 10 minutes, until tunnels appear in the rice. Cover the pan, reduce the heat to low and cook for 5 minutes, until all of the liquid has been absorbed. Fluff the rice with a fork and fold through the lime zest.

Serve the tofu and its poaching liquid over the rice.

Serves 4

500 g firm organic tofu
2 lemongrass stems, halved lengthways
6 kaffir lime leaves, torn
500 ml (2 cups) dashi stock
100 g snow peas
1 bunch of baby bok choy, halved
200 g (1 cup) basmati rice
200 ml coconut milk
finely grated zest of 1 lime

Watermelon mango juice blend

This combo is seriously delicious. I don't use a juicer as it makes me too sad to see all of that beneficial fibre going to waste. Instead, I use a blender. Juice away in summer, but put the handbrake on juices once you pull out your jumpers – it's time for warmer drinks then. I sometimes add a bit of warming turmeric or ginger to my juices to help my digestive system out.

Put the watermelon, mango, lemongrass and mint into a blender and blend until smooth. Pour into glasses and serve.

Serves 4

700 g (4 cups) chopped, chilled watermelon
2 mangoes (about 400 g), peeled and chopped
1 young stalk lemongrass, white part only, chopped
a handful of mint leaves

I love Vietnam chicken patties

Line a baking tray with baking paper.

To make the paste, put the lemongrass, shallots, coriander roots and stems and garlic into a mortar and pestle and pound the living daylights out of them. (Put on your favourite music to do this!)

Transfer the paste to a bowl, add the chicken mince, egg white, fish sauce and a couple of cracks of pepper. Shape tablespoons of the mixture into patties, place them on the lined tray, cover with plastic wrap and chill for 2 hours, or as long as you can. The longer you leave the patties, the better the flavour.

Bring the patties to room temperature 30 minutes before cooking.

Preheat the oven to 180°C.

Heat a small amount of oil in a large frying pan over medium heat. Add the patties, in batches, and cook until browned on both sides. Transfer to baking tray to finish cooking in the oven for 10 minutes to stop them drying out in the pan. Serve with lime wedges.

Makes about 20

3 lemongrass stems, pale part only, chopped
3 red Asian shallots, peeled and coarsely chopped
roots and stems from 1 bunch of coriander, roots scrubbed
2 garlic cloves, coarsely chopped
500 g organic chicken mince (use organic mince with a bit of fat or the patties will be dry)
1 free-range egg white, lightly beaten
1 tablespoon fish sauce
cracked black pepper
coconut oil, for frying
lime wedges, to serve

Avocado with nori and soba

Cook the soba noodles in a large saucepan of boiling water until just soft. Drain under cold running water, then set aside in iced water to chill while you prepare the dressing.

Whisk together the tamari, mirin, lime juice, olive oil and sugar.

Drain the noodles and toss with the sprouts and baby kale, then pour over the dressing.

Divide the noodle mixture between four serving bowls. Top with the avocado and sprinkle with the seeds and shredded nori.

Serves 4

100 g buckwheat soba noodles
2 tablespoons tamari
1 tablespoon mirin
1 tablespoon lime juice
1 tablespoon olive oil
2 teaspoons coconut sugar
50 g mixed sprouts
50 g baby kale
2 avocados, halved
3 tablespoons mixed pepitas, sunflower seeds and linseeds (flaxseeds)
2 nori sheets, shredded

dinner

Watermelon, feta and mint salad with sumac prawns

Watermelon is the perfect summer fruit, as it is incredibly cooling. Here it does a great job of tempering the heat in the salty feta and prawns. I buy watermelon with seeds because I believe it has a better flavour than the seedless type.

Combine the prawns, garlic and oil in a large bowl. Cover and refrigerate for at least 1 hour, or until you are ready to cook. Allow 15 minutes to bring the prawns to room temperature before cooking.

Heat the barbecue chargrill plate or large non-stick frying pan to medium–hot. Cook the prawns for 3–5 minutes, until pink and tender.

Arrange the watermelon, feta and mint leaves on a platter, top with the prawns and pomegranate seeds, then drizzle with the pomegranate molasses. Sprinkle on the sumac and serve with the lime wedges.

Serves 4–6

500 g raw prawns, peeled and deveined, tails left intact
2 garlic cloves, crushed
1 tablespoon olive oil
750 g peeled watermelon, cut into large wedges
100 g Bulgarian goat's feta, crumbled
a handful of mint leaves
seeds of 1 pomegranate
pomegranate molasses, to drizzle
sumac, to sprinkle
lime wedges, to serve

Quinoa tabouleh

Rinse the quinoa under running water, then cook in a large saucepan of boiling water until the tails start to separate from the grain. Rinse under cold water, drain well. Set aside to cool.

Put the spring onion, herbs, tomatoes, sprouted chickpeas, sunflower sprouts and quinoa into a bowl and mix well.

Whisk together the lemon juice, garlic and oil. Pour over the salad and mix to combine. Cover and allow to rest for 1 hour before serving in the lettuce leaves.

Serves 4–6

100 g (½ cup) tricolour quinoa
2 spring onions, finely chopped
2 large handfuls of flat-leaf parsley leaves, roughly chopped
a large handful of mint leaves, roughly chopped
200 g cherry tomatoes, sliced
100 g sprouted chickpeas
100 g sunflower sprouts
3 tablespoons lemon juice
2 garlic cloves, crushed
3 tablespoons extra virgin olive oil
crisp cos or iceberg lettuce leaves, to serve

Charred chicken with chimichurri sauce

Put the chicken into a bowl, add the garlic, ground coriander and olive oil and mix to coat the chicken. Cover and marinate overnight in the fridge, if time allows.

Bring the chicken to room temperature 30 minutes before you are ready to start cooking.

To make the chimichurri sauce, combine the herbs in a bowl, add the garlic, vinegar, oregano, chilli and olive oil and mix well. Set aside while you cook the chicken.

Heat a barbecue or large non-stick frying pan to medium–hot. Cook the marinated chicken for 10 minutes, until charred and cooked through.

Add cooked chicken to the chimichurri sauce and toss to coat.

Serve with the salad and asparagus.

Serves 4–6

500 g free-range chicken thigh fillets, trimmed and halved
2 garlic cloves, chopped
1 teaspoon ground coriander
1 tablespoon olive oil

Chimichurri sauce
2 large handfuls of flat-leaf parsley leaves, chopped
2 large handfuls of coriander leaves, chopped
2 garlic cloves, crushed
2 tablespoons red wine vinegar
1 teaspoon dried oregano
1 long red chilli, seeded and thinly sliced
125 ml (½ cup) extra virgin olive oil

green salad, to serve
barbecued asparagus, to serve

Zucchini, pea and ricotta fritters with garlic tahini yoghurt

Put the zucchini into a colander, sprinkle with salt and allow to stand for 20 minutes. Rinse under cold water to remove the salt, then drain really well, squeezing to remove any excess liquid.

Combine the zucchini, peas, ricotta, spring onion, herbs, flour and eggs in a bowl and mix to combine.

Heat 1 tablespoon of oil in a large frying pan over medium heat, then spoon in a heaped tablespoon of batter per fritter and cook in batches of four for 2–3 minutes on each side until golden brown and cooked through. Drain on a plate lined with paper towel. Cook the remaining fritters.

To make the garlic tahini yoghurt, whisk the tahini, lemon juice, garlic, yoghurt and 1 tablespoon of water in a bowl.

To make the salad, place the avocado, lime and coriander in a bowl and mix to combine.

Serve the fritters with the avocado, lime and coriander salad and the garlic tahini yoghurt drizzled over the top.

Serves 4

2 zucchini, grated
pinch of salt
140 g (1 cup) frozen peas
100 g ricotta, broken into bite-sized pieces
3 spring onions, thinly sliced
a handful of dill, chopped
a handful of flat-leaf parsley leaves, chopped
a handful of mint leaves, chopped
3 tablespoons quinoa flour
2 free-range eggs, lightly beaten
olive oil, for frying

Garlic tahini yoghurt
1 tablespoon hulled tahini
1 tablespoon lemon juice
1 garlic clove, crushed
2 tablespoons Greek-style yoghurt

Avocado, lime and coriander salad
2 avocados, chopped
juice of 1 lime
a handful of coriander leaves

Salt is heating, so limit the amount you add to your food in summer, especially if you are a Pitta type. Take the time to rinse the zucchini well after salting to remove all of the salt.

Fish masala

This is a delicious and simple south Indian fish curry. Like all curries, it is best made ahead of time and reheated. I make the curry sauce and leave it for a few hours, then add the fish when I am about to serve.

Heat the oil in a saucepan over medium heat, add the onion and cook for 10 minutes, until golden. Stir in the coriander and fennel seeds and cook for 3 minutes, until fragrant. Add the garam masala, chilli powder, turmeric and curry leaves and cook for 5 minutes, until the oil separates from the spices.

Stir the coconut milk, salt, tamarind and 125 ml (½ cup) of water into the pan and simmer for 20 minutes, until the oil separates from the sauce. Add the fish, beans, zucchini and tomatoes and simmer for 10 minutes, until the fish is just tender.

Serves 4–6

3 tablespoons coconut oil
1 red onion, finely chopped
1 tablespoon ground coriander
½ teaspoon fennel seeds
1 teaspoon garam masala
½ teaspoon chilli powder
½ teaspoon turmeric
6 fresh curry leaves
400 ml can coconut milk
½ teaspoon sea salt
1 tablespoon tamarind concentrate
750 g firm white fish fillets
   (such as mackerel or mahi mahi)
200 g green beans, trimmed
1 zucchini, sliced
100 g cherry tomatoes

Indonesian turmeric chicken

Turmeric is considered to be tridoshic, making it suitable for all doshas: Pitta, Vata and Kapha. I am often accused of putting it in everything. It is so incredibly therapeutic, why shouldn't I?

Pound the turmeric, lemongrass, coriander root, garlic and peppercorns in a mortar and pestle to form a smooth paste. Transfer to a bowl, add the kecap manis, fish sauce and chicken and mix well. Cover and place in the fridge to marinate overnight.

Bring the chicken to room temperature 30 minutes before you are ready to start cooking.

Preheat the oven to 200°C.

Transfer the chicken to a baking dish and bake for 20 minutes, until golden brown and cooked through. Serve with the jasmine rice and Asian greens.

Serves 4

5 cm piece of fresh turmeric, scraped with
   a teaspoon to remove the skin,
   coarsely chopped
2 lemongrass stems, pale part only,
   coarsely chopped
2 tablespoons coriander roots, scrubbed
1 garlic bulb, cloves separated, peeled
1 teaspoon black peppercorns
1 tablespoon kecap manis
2 teaspoons fish sauce
500 g free-range chicken thigh fillets
steamed jasmine rice, to serve
steamed Asian greens, to serve

Almost raw salad

There is a huge swing towards raw food, but I recommend eating raw vegetables only in hot climates and only if you have a good, strong digestive system.

Layer the vegetables and nuts in serving bowls.

Whisk together the garlic, mustard, pomegranate molasses, lemon juice, maple syrup and olive oil and pour over each salad.

Serves 4–6

There is a belief in traditional medicine that we have a digestive fire and it needs to be kept burning, raw foods are believed to temper that fire and slow down digestion.

50 g baby rocket
200 g broccoli, cut into florets and steamed
2 carrots, grated
2 beetroot, grated
2 zucchini, grated
30 g (¼ cup) roughly chopped pecans
1 garlic clove, crushed
1 tablespoon dijon mustard
1 tablespoon pomegranate molasses
1 tablespoon lemon juice
2 teaspoons pure maple syrup
3 tablespoons olive oil

Warm roast vegetable, chickpea and quinoa salad

Preheat the oven to 200°C.

Put the quinoa and 250 ml (1 cup) of water in a saucepan over high heat and bring to the boil. Cook for 15 minutes, until the tails start to separate from the grain, then drain well. Allow to cool slightly, then fluff with a fork.

Meanwhile, put the red onion, capsicum, carrot, zucchini and chickpeas on a baking tray and roast for 30 minutes. Add the broccoli, return to the oven and roast for 15 minutes more, until the vegetables are tender.

Transfer the quinoa to a bowl, add the kale or spinach and fold in the roast vegetables.

Whisk together the dressing ingredients, pour over the quinoa salad and gently toss to coat.

Serves 4

100 g (½ cup) red quinoa, rinsed
1 red onion, cut into thick wedges
1 red capsicum, cut into thick strips
2 carrots, cut into thick matchsticks
2 zucchini, cut into thick rings
400 g can chickpeas, rinsed and drained
200 g broccoli
100 g baby kale or spinach

Dressing
1 tablespoon pomegranate molasses
1 tablespoon apple cider vinegar
1 tablespoon hulled tahini, at room temperature
1 tablespoon extra virgin olive oil

Coconut and kale dhal

I consider dhal to be a medicine: it stimulates the digestive fire
and cools the body. It is very soothing for the digestive system
and is recommended for people with irritable bowel syndrome
(IBS) or diverticulitis. I like to serve my dhal with basmati rice, as
they do in India. Mung beans are an easily digested protein that
are used a lot in Ayurvedic cooking. If you have trouble finding
them at health food stores, you can always use red lentils, but
they don't have the same therapeutic qualities and are heating
rather than cooling.

Soak mung beans in cold water for 2 hours, rinse and drain well.

Put the mung beans, coconut oil, turmeric, cumin, fennel, ginger,
coconut and 1 litre (4 cups) of water into a saucepan over high
heat and bring to the boil. Reduce the heat to low and simmer
for 20 minutes, until the dhal is soft and most of the water has
been absorbed.

Stir in the kale and cook until it wilts. Remove from the heat, stir in
the lemon juice, ghee, coriander and lightly season with black salt.

Serves 4

210 g (1 cup) split mung beans (moong dal)
1 teaspoon coconut oil
½ teaspoon turmeric
1 teaspoon ground cumin
½ teaspoon ground fennel
1 teaspoon finely grated fresh ginger
15 g (¼ cup) shredded coconut
100 g kale, stems trimmed, leaves shredded
juice of 1 lemon
1 tablespoon ghee (page 122)
2 tablespoons chopped coriander leaves
pinch of black salt

Herbed hummus

Put the chickpeas, tahini, lemon juice, garlic, salt, kale, mint
and coriander into a small food processor and process to
form a smooth paste. With the motor running, gradually add
2–3 tablespoons of iced water and process until the hummus
is light and creamy.

Serves 4

400 g can chickpeas, rinsed and drained
1 tablespoon hulled tahini
1 tablespoon lemon juice
1 garlic clove, crushed
pinch of sea salt
a handful of baby kale leaves, coarsely chopped
a handful of mint leaves, coarsely chopped
a handful of coriander leaves, coarsely chopped

Madjara

Wash the chickpeas, ensuring any that float to the surface are discarded, then drain well. Wash and drain the rice separately.

Put the chickpeas into a saucepan, cover with water and cook over medium heat for 30 minutes, until just soft. Drain well.

Heat the oil in a large saucepan over medium heat, add the onion and cook, stirring occasionally, for 15 minutes, until the onion is dark brown and caramelised. Remove half of the onion from the pan and reserve to garnish.

Add the spices to the pan, with a splash more oil if the pan is dry, and cook for 1 minute, until the spices are fragrant. Add the rice and 1 litre (4 cups) of water, bring to the boil and cook over high heat for 10 minutes. Stir in the chickpeas and cook for 10 minutes more, until the liquid is absorbed and the rice is just tender. Remove from the heat, cover and allow to stand for 10 minutes.

Fluff the madjara with a fork and serve, topped with the reserved caramelised onion.

Serves 6

200 g (1 cup) dried chickpeas
300 g (1½ cups) basmati rice
3 tablespoons olive oil
4 red onions, cut into thin wedges
1 teaspoon turmeric
1 teaspoon ground coriander
1 teaspoon ground cumin
1 teaspoon ground cinnamon

Felafel

Put the chickpeas, broad beans, cumin, ground coriander, chickpea flour, lemon juice and coriander leaves into a food processor and process until the mixture comes together to form a rough paste.

Using wet hands, shape tablespoons of the chickpea mixture into patties.

Heat a little oil in a large frying pan over medium heat, cook the patties in batches of four for 5 minutes, until crisp and golden on both sides. Drain on paper towel.

Serve the felafel with the hummus, madjara and tabouleh.

Serves 4

400 g can chickpeas, rinsed and drained
155 g (1 cup) frozen broad beans,
   thawed and peeled
1 teaspoon ground cumin
1 teaspoon ground coriander
1 tablespoon chickpea flour (besan)
1 tablespoon lemon juice
3 tablespoons chopped coriander leaves
olive oil, for shallow frying
Herbed hummus (page 62), to serve
Madjara (above), to serve
Quinoa tabouleh (page 52), to serve

treats

Fruit salad with coconut fennel sprinkle

Layer the rockmelon, papaya, kiwi fruit, watermelon, strawberries and blueberries on a large plate. Drizzle with the lime juice.

To make the coconut fennel sprinkle, put the coconut, fennel seeds and saffron threads into a small non-stick frying pan, add 1 tablespoon of water and cook over medium heat for 5 minutes, until the coconut is dry and the fennel is toasted.

Scatter the coconut fennel sprinkle over the grated fruit salad just before serving.

Serves 4–6

½ small rockmelon, sliced
1 small red papaya, sliced
4 kiwi fruit, grated
300 g peeled watermelon, sliced
100 g strawberries, grated
100 g blueberries
juice of 2 limes

Coconut fennel sprinkle
30 g (⅓ cup) desiccated coconut
2 teaspoons fennel seeds
pinch of saffron threads

Coconut tapioca with papaya and lime

I make tapioca regularly – and regularly burn the bottom of my pan in the process. So this recipe comes with a stirring warning.

Papaya is warming; here, I use lime to cool it down. Use any tropical fruit that is available, but don't forget the lime – there is a reason they are always served together in the tropics.

Put the tapioca and coconut cream into a saucepan, add 500 ml (2 cups) of water and allow to stand for 30 minutes.

Add the kaffir lime leaves, vanilla bean and seeds to the tapioca mixture in the pan and cook, stirring occasionally, over medium heat until the tapioca comes to the boil. Reduce the heat to low and simmer, stirring several times to stop the mixture from catching on the bottom of the pan, for 10 minutes, until the pearls are soft. Remove the pan from the heat, stir in the brown rice syrup and remove the vanilla bean.

Divide the coconut tapioca between four serving glasses, top with the chopped papaya and lime zest and serve.

Serves 4

145 g (¾ cup) tapioca pearls
400 ml coconut cream
6 kaffir lime leaves, torn
1 vanilla bean, split lengthways and seeds scraped
3 tablespoons brown rice syrup
½ small red papaya, finely chopped
finely grated zest of 1 lime

Fig tart with maple yoghurt

Grease and line a 20 cm springform cake tin.

To make the maple yoghurt, put the yoghurt into a bowl, add the maple syrup and vanilla and mix to combine. Suspend a fine sieve over a bowl. Line the sieve with a double layer of muslin or a tea towel, add the yoghurt mixture and twist to enclose, tying the top with kitchen string or an elastic band. Refrigerate overnight. The longer you leave the yoghurt to drain, the firmer it will be.

Put the chopped dates and almonds into a food processor and process until the mixture resembles fine breadcrumbs. Add the tahini, ginger and cinnamon, then process until the mixture just comes together.

Press the date mixture into the prepared cake tin, spread the maple yoghurt over the top and refrigerate for 4 hours. Remove from the tin, top with the figs and serve.

Serves 6–8

250 g pitted medjool dates, coarsely chopped
60 g whole almonds, coarsely chopped
1 tablespoon hulled tahini
1 teaspoon ground ginger
1 teaspoon ground cinnamon
8 figs, torn in half

Maple yoghurt
500 g Greek-style yoghurt
2 teaspoons pure maple syrup
1 teaspoon natural vanilla extract

Yoghurt pearls with saffron syrup

Put the saffron threads into a small saucepan, add the sugar and 250 ml (1 cup) of water and stir over low heat until the sugar has dissolved. Bring to the boil over high heat and cook, without stirring, for 10 minutes, until the syrup has reduced by half. Set the syrup aside to cool.

Combine the sunflower seeds, pepitas and pecans on a plate.

With wet hands, roll tablespoons of the yoghurt cheese into walnut-sized balls. Roll the balls in the seed and nut mixture. Serve the yoghurt pearls in a small pool of the saffron syrup.

Serves 4

pinch of saffron threads
2 tablespoons raw sugar
500 g Yoghurt cheese (page 100)
2 tablespoons sunflower seeds
2 tablespoons pepitas
2 tablespoons finely chopped pecans

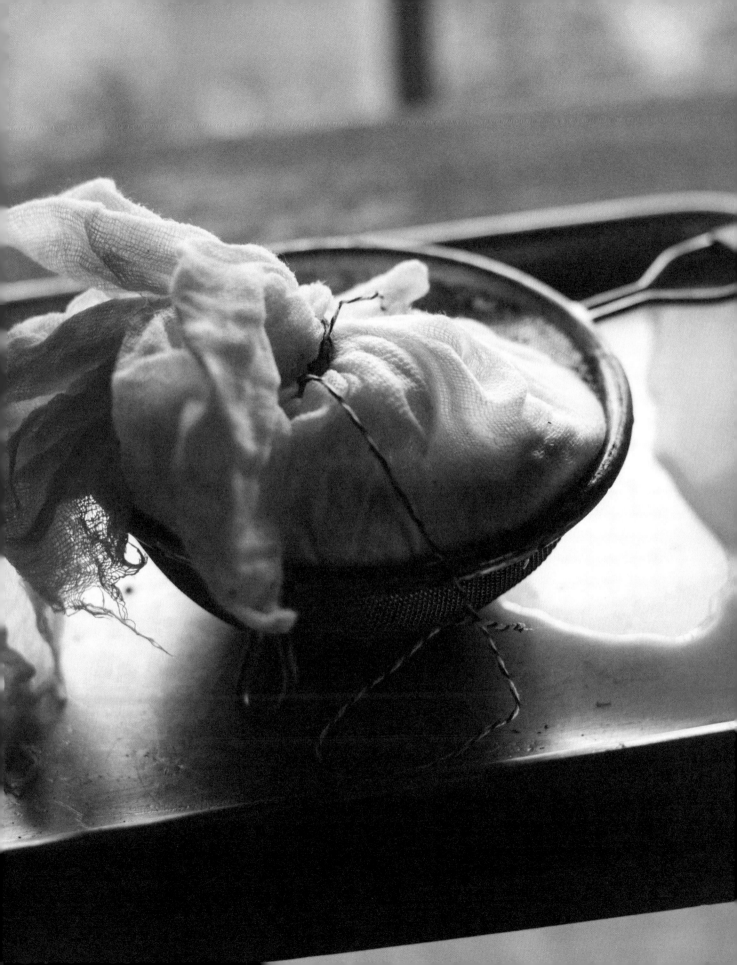

Rosewater and pistachio cake

This gluten-free cake is adapted from the Rose Bakery recipe in *Breakfast Lunch Tea*, one of my most cherished books. My all-time favourite cake, the rosewater makes it taste so exotic. I am yet to serve this to anyone who hasn't loved it.

Preheat the oven to 180°C. Grease and line an 8 cm x 22 cm loaf tin with baking paper.

Cream the butter and sugar until pale and creamy, add the lemon zest and rosewater and beat to combine. Gradually add the eggs, beating well after each addition. Fold in a couple of tablespoons of the ground pistachios to prevent the mixture curdling, then fold in the remaining ground pistachios and the almond meal. Pour the mixture into the prepared tin and bake for 45 minutes, until a skewer inserted in the centre of the cake comes out clean. Place on a wire rack and cool in the tin.

To make the syrup, put the lemon zest and juice into a small saucepan, add the sugar and stir over low heat until the sugar dissolves. Bring to the boil and cook, without stirring, over high heat until the syrup is reduced by half.

Pour the hot syrup over the cold cake (or the cold syrup over the hot cake) for the best absorption.

Decorate with the pomegranate seeds, mint leaves and coarsely chopped pistachios and serve with the coconut yoghurt.

Serves 8

Being quiet and still is one of the most cooling things you can do.

250 g butter, softened
140 g (⅔ cup) coconut sugar
finely grated zest of 1 lemon
2 tablespoons rosewater
4 free-range eggs, lightly beaten
160 g ground unsalted pistachio nuts
100 g (1 cup) almond meal
seeds of 1 pomegranate
a small handful of mint leaves
50 g coarsely chopped unsalted
   pistachio nuts, to serve
coconut yoghurt, to serve

Syrup
finely grated zest and juice of 2 lemons
90 g (½ cup) coconut sugar

Strawberry, almond and rose friands

Preheat the oven to 190°C. Grease six 125 ml (½ cup) friand tins and line with baking paper.

Put the almond meal, icing sugar, cornflour, flour and baking powder into a bowl and mix to combine. Stir in the egg whites, rosewater, cinnamon, lemon zest and oil. Divide the mixture between the prepared tins and top with the sliced strawberries and almonds. Bake for 20 minutes, until a skewer inserted in the centre of a friand comes out clean. Transfer to a wire rack and allow to cool in the tins. Dust with the extra icing sugar to serve.

Makes 6

150 g (1½ cups) almond meal
60 g (½ cup) icing sugar, plus extra for dusting
140 g (⅓ cup) cornflour
30 g (¼ cup) gluten-free plain flour
½ teaspoon gluten-free baking powder
5 free-range egg whites
2 teaspoons rosewater
½ teaspoon ground cinnamon
finely grated zest of 1 lemon
100 ml olive oil
5 strawberries, thinly sliced
10 whole almonds, sliced

Cooling rose and vanilla chai

Cooling milky teas are quite refreshing in summer, especially if you are a hot Pitta type. If cow's milk is not your thing, then this is delicious with homemade almond milk or organic soy milk.

Using a mortar and pestle, pound the rosebuds until roughly crushed, then transfer to a large saucepan.

Coarsely crush the fennel seeds and cardamom in the mortar and pestle. Don't go crazy – you don't want a powder. Add to the pan, along with the cinnamon sticks and vanilla bean and seeds. Pour in 2 litres (8 cups) of water and bring to the boil over high heat. Reduce the heat to low and simmer for 1 hour, until the liquid has reduced by half and is a deep brown colour.

Add the milk to the pan and simmer for 30 minutes. Strain and cool. Serve warm or chilled.

Serves 4

8 dried edible rosebuds
1 teaspoon fennel seeds
½ teaspoon green cardamom pods
2 cinnamon sticks, halved
1 vanilla bean, split in half lengthways and
  seeds scraped
500 ml (2 cups) unhomogenised organic milk
  or milk of your choice

Coconut berry frozen lollies

Put the coconut cream and maple syrup into a jug and mix.

Divide the raspberries and blueberries among 6 ice-block moulds. Pour in the coconut mixture, then insert an ice-cream stick in the centre and freeze until firm.

Makes 6

300 ml coconut cream
1 teaspoon pure maple syrup
100 g raspberries
50 g blueberries

Indonesian chocolate avocado smoothie

Okay, I know this sounds weird, but it truly is amazing. I first got hooked on it while travelling in Indonesia. The original recipe used condensed milk but I just can't bring myself to start the day with that kind of sugar hit.

Put the banana, avocado, cacao, maple syrup (if using) and milk into a blender and blend until smooth.

Serves 4

1 banana, chopped
1 avocado, chopped
1–2 teaspoons cacao powder (depending on how chocolatey you want your smoothie)
1 tablespoon pure maple syrup (optional – you won't need this if you use a ripe banana)
1 litre (4 cups) chilled rice milk

Sparkling mango pops

Crush the mint leaves in a mortar and pestle, then stir in the mineral water.

Divide the mixture between 6 ice-block moulds, insert an ice-cream stick in the centre, then freeze until just firm.

Put the mango and strawberries into a bowl and gently swirl to combine. Pour onto the frozen mint mixture in the moulds. Freeze until firm.

Makes 6

6 mint leaves, torn
3 tablespoons sparkling mineral water
1 mango, pureed
100 g small strawberries, hulled and lightly crushed

Dates filled with rosewater cheese and pistachios

Put the yoghurt cheese and rosewater into a bowl and combine.

Split the dates and remove the seeds, taking care not to cut all the way through the middle.

Fill the centre of each date with the rosewater cheese, then sprinkle with the pistachios.

Makes 12

125 g yoghurt cheese (page 100)
1 teaspoon rosewater
12 medjool dates
2 tablespoons finely chopped unsalted pistachio nuts

Spirulina, vanilla and almond protein balls

Put the whole almonds and quinoa flakes into a food processor and process until the mixture resembles coarse breadcrumbs. Add the tahini, chia seeds, rice syrup, vanilla extract and spirulina. Process until the mixture comes together and starts to leave the side of the bowl.

Shape heaped teaspoons of the mixture into balls. Roll in the chopped almonds. Store in an airtight container for up to 7 days.

Makes about 16

200 g (1¼ cups) whole almonds, soaked overnight in cold water and drained
50 g (½ cup) quinoa flakes
2 tablespoons hulled tahini
1 tablespoon white chia seeds
1 tablespoon brown rice syrup
1 teaspoon natural vanilla extract
1 teaspoon spirulina powder
finely chopped almonds, for coating

Banana, macadamia and chocolate bliss balls

Put the dates and almonds into a small food processor and process until the mixture resembles breadcrumbs. Add the nut butter, cacao, banana and coconut and process until the mixture comes together and starts to leave the side of the bowl.

Roll heaped teaspoons of the mixture into balls, then roll in coconut. Store in an airtight container for up to 7 days.

Makes about 16

250 g pitted medjool dates, coarsely chopped
50 g whole almonds, soaked overnight in cold water and drained
1 tablespoon macadamia butter or any nut butter
1 tablespoon cacao powder
1 banana, coarsely chopped
2 tablespoons desiccated coconut, plus extra for rolling

Elderflower and saffron panna cotta with strawberry mint crush

Grease four 125 ml (½ cup) dariole moulds with coconut oil.

Put 2 tablespoons of boiling water into a jug, stir in the saffron threads and set aside to cool slightly but not completely – about 5 minutes, or the gelatine won't melt. Strain the liquid, sprinkle over the gelatine and whisk until the gelatine is dissolved. Cool.

Put the yoghurt into a bowl, add the maple syrup, elderflower cordial and vanilla and mix to combine.

Stir the cooled saffron gelatine into the yoghurt mixture.

Divide the mixture between the prepared moulds, cover with plastic wrap, place on a tray and transfer to the fridge to chill for 4 hours, until set.

Run a flat-bladed knife gently around the outside of each panna cotta to loosen, then invert onto a serving plate.

Crush the mint leaves with the raw sugar in a mortar and pestle, then fold into the strawberries. Use to garnish each panna cotta.

Serves 4

coconut oil, for greasing
pinch of saffron threads
2 teaspoons powdered gelatine
520 g (2 cups) organic Greek-style yoghurt
1 tablespoon pure maple syrup
1 tablespoon elderflower cordial
1 teaspoon natural vanilla extract
2 tablespoons mint leaves
2 tablespoons raw sugar
200 g strawberries, hulled and sliced

Minty elderflower, peach and lychee tea

Put the tea bags into a large jug, pour over 250 ml (1 cup) of boiling water and allow to steep for 30 minutes, until cool. Remove the tea bags.

Slice the tops off the coconuts using a cleaver. Pour out the coconut water and reserve, then scoop out big strips of the flesh with a spoon.

Add the coconut water, coconut flesh, peaches, lychees, mint, elderflower cordial and 1 litre (4 cups) of chilled water to the peppermint tea and stir to combine.

Serves 4

3 peppermint tea bags
2 fresh young coconuts
2 peaches, thinly sliced
100 g lychees, peeled and sliced
a handful of mint leaves
3 tablespoons elderflower cordial

FOODS THAT GROUND
for unsettled days

ADZUKI BEANS, ALMONDS, APPLES, BASMATI RICE, BEETROOT, CARROT, CASHEWS, CELERIAC, COOKED FRUIT, DAIKON, FIGS, GARLIC, GHEE, KOHLRABI, LEEK, ONION, PARSNIP, PEARS, PUMPKIN, SESAME SEEDS, SPRING ONION, SQUASH, SWEET POTATO, WALNUTS, WHOLE DAIRY, ADZUKI BEANS, ALMONDS, APPLES, BASMATI RICE, BEETROOT, CARROT, CASHEWS, CELERIAC, COOKED FRUIT, DAIKON, FIGS, GARLIC, GHEE, KOHLRABI, LEEK, ONION, PARSNIP, PEARS, PUMPKIN, SESAME SEEDS, SPRING ONION, SQUASH, SWEET POTATO, WALNUTS, WHOLE DAIRY, ADZUKI BEANS, ALMONDS, APPLES, BASMATI RICE, BEETROOT, CARROT, CASHEWS, CELERIAC, COOKED FRUIT...

breakfast

Vegetable miso soup

When things go slightly pear-shaped for me, I reach for miso. I make a big pot, ensuring it has plenty of grounding vegetables in the mix, and then sip on it all day long. I prefer to use an organic shiro miso made from sweet white rice, but if it is cold and windy, then I use a darker, saltier, brown rice genmai miso.

Put 1.25 litres (5 cups) of water into a large saucepan, add the wakame, spring onion, carrot, daikon, mushroom and ginger and bring to the boil, reduce the heat to low and simmer for 15 minutes.

Blend the miso with 2 tablespoons of the hot stock and add to the pan; do not allow the stock to boil once you have done this. Add the asparagus, edamame and tofu and cook for 5 minutes, until the edamame are bright green and tender.

Serves 4

10 g dried wakame
4 spring onions, thinly sliced
1 carrot, thinly sliced
1 small daikon radish, thinly sliced
6 dried Chinese mushrooms, broken into
  small pieces
5 cm piece of fresh ginger, finely julienned
2 tablespoons shiro miso
6 asparagus spears, woody ends trimmed, sliced
180 g (1 cup) frozen shelled edamame
150 g silken firm tofu, cut into small cubes

Gomasio

Place the salt in a frying pan and toast over medium heat until it turns grey. Transfer the salt to a mortar and pestle – a suribachi (a ridged Japanese mortar and pestle) is ideal – and set aside.

Add the sesame seeds to the pan and cook over medium heat until the seeds start to pop and move around in the pan. Transfer to the mortar and pestle and gently grind with the salt to break up the seeds. You don't want them to be too fine and you don't want to end up with salty tahini.

Transfer the mixture to an airtight container and store for up to 2 months. Sprinkle over soups, salads and roast vegetables.

Makes 75 g (½ cup)

1 tablespoon sea salt
75 g (½ cup) black or white sesame seeds

Comforting congee

This is a savoury version, but I sometimes leave out the savoury flavourings and serve a simple congee with stewed fruit that is in season. You'll need a slow cooker for this recipe.

Toast the drained rice in a large dry frying pan over medium heat until fragrant.

Transfer the rice to a slow cooker, add the kombu, garlic, spring onion, water or dashi, turn the heat to medium and leave to cook overnight.

The next day, if there is a lot of excess liquid, transfer the rice to a large saucepan and cook over high heat until thick and creamy but still soupy. Stir the tamari into the rice.

Blend the miso with 375ml (1½ cups) of hot water, place in a small saucepan over medium heat and cook without boiling for 5 minutes.

Spoon the congee into bowls, then ladle on some of the miso broth. Dot the ghee on top and finish with the gomasio, tamari seeds, fried shallots, egg and torn nori.

Serves 6

220 g (1 cup) medium-grain brown rice, rinsed and drained
1 piece of kombu
1 garlic bulb, halved
4 spring onions, sliced
3 litres (12 cups) water or dashi stock
2 tablespoons tamari
1 tablespoon shiro miso
2 tablespoons ghee (page 122)
3 tablespoons Gomasio (page 84)
3 tablespoons Tamari seeds (see below)
3 tablespoons fried shallots
2 hard-boiled free-range eggs, grated (optional)
1 nori sheet, torn into small pieces

Tamari seeds

Put the seeds into a large frying pan and cook over medium heat for 5 minutes, until nice and brown. Add the tamari and toss to coat the seeds, then reduce the heat to low and cook until the seeds are dry.

Allow the seeds to cool before storing in an airtight container.

Makes 210 g (2 cups)

210 g (2 cups) mixed sunflower seeds, pepitas, linseeds (flaxseeds)
2 tablespoons tamari

Grilled figs on honeyed nut butter with spiced nuts

Sweet juicy fruits are very grounding, especially those with seeds, and are best served warm on windy, unsettled mornings. This recipe is also delicious with poached dried figs.

Preheat the grill to medium.

Tear the figs in half and place on a baking tray lined with baking paper. Place a small piece of ghee in the centre of each fig. Cook under the grill until the figs are warmed through and the ghee has melted.

Fold the honey through the super spread or nut butter, then spread some of the honeyed paste on each serving plate.

To make the spiced nuts, put the walnuts, pine nuts and cinnamon into a bowl and mix to combine.

Top the honeyed nut butter with the figs, sprinkle with the spiced nuts and finish with a little honeycomb and some pink peppercorns.

Serves 4

8 figs
1 tablespoon ghee (page 122)
2 teaspoons raw honey
4 tablespoons super spread or nut butter
2 tablespoons raw honeycomb
2 teaspoons pink peppercorns, cracked

Spiced nuts
2 tablespoons walnuts
2 tablespoons pine nuts
½ teaspoon ground cinnamon

Fruits and vegetables with seeds and stones help draw us down into our centre. Cooked fruits are more grounding than fresh, which tend to be more cooling.

Sesame and egg fried rice

Heat the ghee and sesame oil in a small frying pan over medium heat, add the spring onion and cook for 3 minutes, until soft.

Pour the egg into the pan and cook until lightly set, then stir to break up and scramble lightly. Add the rice and cook for several minutes, until warmed through. Serve topped with the gomasio and the extra spring onion.

Serves 2

1 tablespoon ghee (page 122)
½ teaspoon sesame oil
3 spring onions, sliced, plus extra to serve
2 free-range eggs, lightly beaten
185 g (1 cup) cooked basmati rice, cooled
¼ teaspoon Gomasio (page 84)

Sweet omelette rolls with pistachio and goji sprinkle

Whisk together the eggs and maple syrup in a bowl.

Heat a little of the ghee in a small frying pan, add 2 tablespoons of the egg mixture and cook over medium heat until the egg is just set around the edge. Sprinkle with some sesame seeds, then gently roll the omelette up in the pan. Transfer to a plate and keep warm. Repeat this process with the remaining egg mixture.

To make the pistachio and goji sprinkle, put the berries, pistachios, sesame seeds and coconut sugar into a bowl and mix to combine.

Scatter the pistachio and goji sprinkle over the omelette rolls and serve immediately.

Serves 4

4 free-range eggs
2 teaspoons pure maple syrup
1 tablespoon ghee (page 122)
1 teaspoon black sesame seeds

Pistachio and goji sprinkle
1 tablespoon goji berries
1 tablespoon unsalted pistachio nuts, coarsely chopped
1 teaspoon black sesame seeds
1 teaspoon coconut sugar

Sweet carrot and ricotta pancakes

Carrot is an incredibly grounding, calming vegetable; in fact, any vegetable that needs to push down into the earth to grow will bring us out of our chatty, busy minds and down into our bodies.

To make the orange, cinnamon and maple butter, put the butter, cardamom, orange zest and maple syrup into a bowl and mix to combine.

Place the butter mixture on a piece of plastic wrap and shape into a log, roll up and chill until firm.

Combine the ricotta, egg yolks and almond milk in a bowl.

In a separate bowl, sift in the flour, baking powder and spices, then stir in the quinoa flakes and almond meal. Make a well in the centre and stir in the ricotta mixture.

Whisk the egg whites in a large bowl until stiff peaks form. Fold into the ricotta mixture with the grated carrot.

Melt a little of the butter in a non-stick frying pan over medium heat and drop 3 tablespoons of batter per pancake into the pan. Cook for 3 minutes, until the underside is golden, turn and cook the other side for another 3 minutes, until golden. Transfer the pancakes to a plate and keep warm in the oven while you cook the remaining pancakes.

Serve the pancakes topped with slices of the orange, cinnamon and maple butter and a good splash of maple syrup.

Serves 4–6

I like to have vegetables at every meal — even breakfast.

250 g fresh ricotta
4 free-range eggs, separated
375 ml (1½ cups) unsweetened almond milk
130 g (1½ cups) buckwheat flour
2 teaspoons gluten-free baking powder
1 teaspoon ground cinnamon
½ teaspoon ground ginger
25 g (½ cup) quinoa flakes
25 g (¼ cup) almond meal
100 g carrot, grated
25 g butter
pure maple syrup, to serve

Orange, cinnamon and maple butter
100 g butter, softened
½ teaspoon ground cardamom
1 teaspoon finely grated orange zest
2 teaspoons pure maple syrup

Carrot halva with warm almond quinoa

This is a great portable breakfast. Instead of the grated carrot, you could top the halva with mixed berries or poached stone fruit – but the grated carrot is something a little different.

In Ayurveda it is recommended that almonds are soaked overnight to make them easier to digest. We even soak our raisins, too, if we have time.

Put the quinoa into a saucepan, cover with plenty of water and cook over high heat for 15 minutes, until the tails separate from the seed. Drain well, stir in the almond milk and keep warm.

Heat the ghee in a large frying pan, add the cardamom and cook over medium heat for 1 minute, until fragrant. Add the carrot and cook for 10 minutes, until soft. Stir in the raisins, almonds and rice syrup and cook until heated through.

Spoon the warm quinoa mixture into four serving glasses and top with the carrot halva.

Serves 4

100 g (½ cup) quinoa, rinsed
500 ml (2 cups) unsweetened almond milk
2 tablespoons ghee (page 122)
4 green cardamom pods, bruised
310 g (2 cups) grated carrot
1 tablespoon raisins
50 g (scant ⅓ cup) whole almonds, soaked overnight, drained and coarsely chopped
2 tablespoons brown rice syrup

Morning poha

This is an Ayurvedic breakfast for those, like me, who prefer a savoury instead of a sweet start to the day. The rice flakes should be cooked in ghee rather than butter because ghee is much more grounding. Overcooking the rice flakes will turn them to mush.

Heat the ghee in a large frying pan over medium heat, add the onion and cook for 5 minutes, until the onion is soft and golden. Stir in the mustard seeds and turmeric and cook until the mustard seeds begin to pop.

Add the carrot, asparagus and rice flakes to the pan and cook for 5 minutes, until the rice flakes are just soft.

Serves 4

1 tablespoon ghee (page 122)
1 onion, grated
1 teaspoon black mustard seeds
pinch of turmeric
1 carrot, grated
6 asparagus spears, woody ends trimmed, chopped
100 g (1 cup) rice flakes

Baby apples with lavender and vanilla

Apples should always be lightly cooked if we are looking to calm and balance Vata or movement. This is because apples are naturally light, crisp and crunchy, and are considered too cooling for anyone with a fragile digestive system. If you feel like a fresh apple, go for sweet and juicy over sour and tart.

Cut around the middle of each apple, taking care not to cut all the way through. This stops the skin from splitting unevenly – it does not need to be a deep cut.

Put the apples in a large saucepan. Add the lavender, vanilla bean and coconut sugar. Cover with water and cook over medium heat for 30 minutes, until the apples are soft.

Serves 4–6

12 small organic sweet red apples
2 lavender sprigs
1 vanilla bean, split lengthways
3 tablespoons coconut sugar

Warm spice-infused almond milk

Put the almond milk into a saucepan, add the ghee, cinnamon stick, orange flower water and ginger and simmer over medium heat for 10 minutes, until the flavours infuse. Set aside to cool slightly (you don't want the liquid to be too hot when you pour it over the honeycomb or it will affect the health-giving properties of the honey). Remove the cinnamon stick.

To serve, place a small piece of the honeycomb in each cup and pour the warm, cinnamon-infused milk over the top.

Serves 2–4

500 ml (2 cups) unsweetened almond milk
1 teaspoon ghee (page 122)
1 cinnamon stick
1 teaspoon orange flower water
3 slices of fresh ginger
1 tablespoon raw honeycomb

lunch

Warm beetroot, ricotta and walnut salad

Preheat the oven to 200°C. Line a baking tray with baking paper.

Put the beetroot and onion into a baking dish, drizzle over half the olive oil and toss to coat. Put the ricotta on the prepared tray, sprinkle with the ras el hanout and drizzle with the remaining olive oil. Place the baking dish and baking tray in the oven and bake for 40 minutes, until the beetroot is soft and the ricotta is golden. When cool enough to handle, halve the beetroot and cut the ricotta into four wedges.

Arrange the spinach leaves on serving plates and top with the beetroot, onion, baked ricotta, pepitas, walnuts and olives.

Whisk together the verjuice, horseradish and extra virgin olive oil. Drizzle over the salad and serve.

Serves 4

12 baby beetroot, scrubbed
1 red onion, cut into thick wedges
1 tablespoon olive oil
400 g fresh ricotta
1 teaspoon ras el hanout
150 g baby spinach leaves
2 tablespoons pepitas
50 g walnuts
60 g green Sicilian olives
2 tablespoons verjuice
2 teaspoons grated horseradish, from a jar
4 tablespoons extra virgin olive oil

Roast sweet potato and carrot with sesame and maple

Preheat the oven to 200°C. Line a baking tray with baking paper.

Put the sweet potatoes and carrots on the prepared tray and roast for 30–40 minutes, until soft.

Split the sweet potatoes in half lengthways and smear the ghee along the cut sides. Top with the carrots. Drizzle with the maple syrup, tamari and sesame oil, sprinkle with the sesame seeds.

Serves 4–6

8 small sweet potatoes, scrubbed
12 baby carrots, scrubbed
1 tablespoon ghee (page 122)
1 tablespoon pure maple syrup
1 tablespoon tamari
1 teaspoon sesame oil
1 tablespoon black sesame seeds

Pumpkin, feta and smoky onion tart

Preheat the oven to 200°C. Place baking tray in the oven to heat.

Put the flours, sesame seeds and salt in a heatproof bowl.

Combine the olive oil and 100 ml of water in a saucepan and bring just to the boil. Pour into the dry ingredients and mix until the dough comes together – it may be a little crumbly.

Press the dough into a 24 cm fluted tart tin, line with baking paper and pour in some baking beads or uncooked rice. Place the tart tin on the heated baking tray (this helps the pastry base cook evenly) and transfer to the oven. Bake for 20 minutes, remove the paper and weights and bake for 15 minutes more, until the pastry is crisp and golden. Reduce the oven temperature to 180°C.

Meanwhile, make the filling. Heat the oil in a large frying pan over medium heat. Add the sliced onion and paprika and cook, stirring occasionally, for 10 minutes, until the onion is sticky and caramelised. Keep an eye on the onion to make sure it doesn't catch and burn. Allow to cool slightly.

Line the cooked pastry base with the onion, then top with scoops of the roast pumpkin, large chunks of the feta and scatter on the rosemary leaves. Pour over the egg and bake for 20 minutes, until the egg is set and the tart is golden.

Serves 4–6

TIP: Take a whole pumpkin in its skin, pop it onto a baking tray and bake in the oven at 180°C until it is really soft, then simply scoop out the flesh.

150 g (1 cup) quinoa flour
100 g (⅔ cup) chickpea flour (besan)
75 g (½ cup) black sesame seeds
pinch of sea salt
100 ml extra virgin olive oil

Filling
2 tablespoons olive oil
4 red onions, thinly sliced
2 teaspoons smoked paprika
250 g roast pumpkin (see Tip)
75 g goat's feta, broken into large chunks
1 tablespoon rosemary leaves
2 free-range eggs, lightly beaten

Super seed crackers

These are the most amazing crackers. I change what I add to them each time I cook them. They can be made into a sweet snack by adding a little maple syrup with the water.

Preheat the oven to 160°C. Line a baking tray with baking paper.

Put the linseeds, mixed seeds, sesame seeds, chia seeds and almond meal into a bowl and mix to combine. Add 250 ml (1 cup) of water and stir until the mixture comes together.

Spread the mixture on the prepared tray (as thickly or thinly as you wish), gently press the salt, nori and pink peppercorns on top and bake for 40 minutes, until crisp. Cut the large cracker in half and turn to cook the other side for 15 minutes, until crisp and dry. Remove from the oven and allow to cool on the tray. Break into bite-sized crackers.

Spoon the yoghurt cheese into a bowl, sprinkle over the dukkah, then drizzle with the extra virgin olive oil. Serve with the crackers.

Serves 4–6

75 g (½ cup) linseeds (flaxseeds)
75 g (½ cup) mixed pepitas and
  sunflower seeds
75 g (½ cup) sesame seeds
70 g (½ cup) chia seeds
50 g (½ cup) almond meal
sea salt, to sprinkle
1 nori sheet
1 tablespoon pink peppercorns
Yoghurt cheese (see below), to serve
Hazelnut dukkah (page 103), to serve
extra virgin olive oil, to serve

Yoghurt cheese

Straining yoghurt overnight removes a large amount of moisture and leaves you with a thick yoghurt cream that makes a perfect tart filling. The longer you leave it hanging, the thicker it will become. You can roll balls of the thickened yoghurt in chopped nuts and serve them as a simple snack.

Suspend a fine sieve over a bowl. Line the sieve with a double layer of muslin or a clean tea towel, spoon in the yoghurt and twist to enclose, tying the top with kitchen string or an elastic band. Refrigerate overnight. Leave in the muslin for a few days if you want your yoghurt cheese to be really dry, otherwise store it in some olive oil with some spices or just keep in an airtight container in the fridge for 1 to 2 weeks.

Makes 450 g

500 g organic Greek-style yoghurt

Kasoundi

This is my all-time favourite Indian pickle. I vary the recipe, using onions, capsicums, tomatoes and even apple and mango I have lying around. It's amazing with Super seed crackers (page 100) and delicious as a base for vegetable curry with coconut milk.

Preheat the oven to 100°C. Wash four 500 ml (2 cup) glass preserving jars in hot, soapy water, then rinse. Place the jars upside down on a baking tray and transfer to the oven to dry. After 10 minutes, invert and continue to heat until the jars are completely dry.

Heat the oil in a large stockpot, add the onion and cook, stirring occasionally, over medium heat for 10 minutes, until soft. Stir in the spices and cook for 3 minutes, until they start to pop. Add the garlic and ginger and cook for 3 minutes, until fragrant.

Add the capsicum, tomato and salt and cook, stirring now and then, over low heat for 30 minutes, until soft but still chunky. Stir in the vinegar and sugar and cook for 30 minutes more, until the pickle is thick and most of the liquid has evaporated. You can check if it is ready by dragging a large wooden spoon through the middle, if no liquid runs into the line created, it is ready to bottle.

Remove the kasoundi from the heat and pour into the jars. Store in a cool, dry place for up to 12 months. Refrigerate after opening.

Makes 4 x 500 ml (2 cup) jars

3 tablespoons olive oil
3 red onions, chopped
1 tablespoon cumin seeds
1 tablespoon yellow mustard seeds
1 tablespoon grated fresh or 2 teaspoons
  dried turmeric
6 garlic cloves, chopped
2 tablespoons grated fresh ginger
6 small red capsicums, chopped
2 kg ripe tomatoes, chopped
2 teaspoons sea salt
250 ml (1 cup) apple cider vinegar
250 g (1 cup) coconut sugar

Yoghurt-spiced beetroot dip

Preheat the oven to 180°C.

Wrap the beetroot in foil and roast for 40 minutes, until tender. Allow to cool, then peel and coarsely chop.

Place the beetroot, garlic, ras el hanout and yoghurt in a food processor and whiz until smooth. Spoon into a bowl and serve.

Makes 260 g (1 cup)

2 small beetroot, scrubbed
1 garlic clove, chopped
½ teaspoon ras el hanout
130 g (½ cup) Greek-style yoghurt

Hazelnut dukkah

Put the coriander seeds into a frying pan and cook over medium heat for 3 minutes, until the seeds start to pop and move around in the pan. Transfer to a mortar and pestle or spice grinder.

Add the cumin seeds and sesame seeds to the pan and toast over medium heat for 3 minutes, until they begin to pop. Tip into the mortar and pestle or spice grinder and lightly crush to a coarse powder. Stir in the paprika and salt. Add the chopped nuts and mix to combine.

Store the dukkah in an airtight container for up to 1 month.

Makes 110 g (1 cup)

2 tablespoons coriander seeds
2 tablespoons cumin seeds
2 tablespoons sesame seeds
1 teaspoon sweet paprika
½ teaspoon garlic sea salt
60 g (½ cup) hazelnuts, toasted and chopped
2 tablespoons pistachio nuts, coarsely chopped

Herbed paneer

Put the milk and garlic into a saucepan and cook over medium heat until the milk is just about to boil. Stir in the lemon juice and cook, stirring constantly, for 10 minutes, until the milk separates into curds and whey.

Place a sieve lined with muslin or a clean tea towel over a bowl, pour in the paneer mixture, add the herbs and mix to combine. Bring the corners of the cloth together and twist to remove any excess liquid. Set aside to drain for 30 minutes to 1 hour, depending on how firm you prefer your paneer to be. (Whey from unflavoured paneer is rich in protein and can be used in smoothies or cakes.)

Use the paneer in curries or soups or cook with spinach to make palak paneer.

Serves 4

500 ml (2 cups) unhomogenised organic milk
2 garlic cloves, peeled
juice of 1 lemon
2 tablespoons finely chopped flat-leaf parsley
2 tablespoons snipped chives

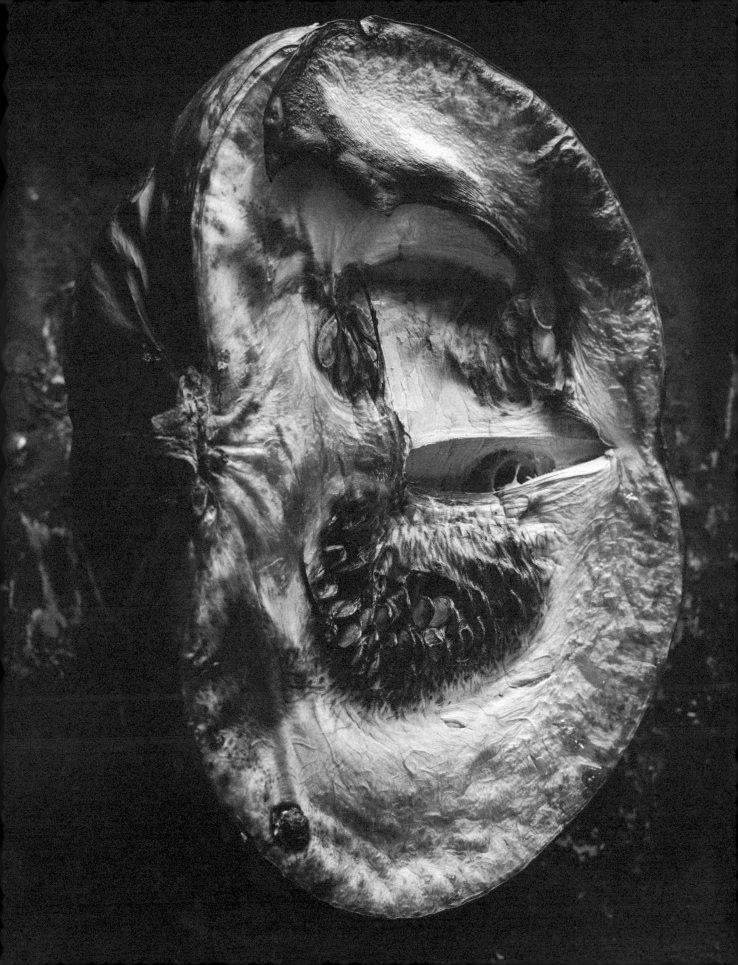

Savoury pumpkin, pepita and pepper scones

These scones are great served with soup as a substitute for bread.

Preheat the oven to 220°C. Line a baking tray with baking paper.

Sift the flours and baking powder into a bowl, stir in the polenta, spring onion and salt. Make a well in the centre. In a separate bowl, combine the pumpkin, yoghurt and olive oil. Stir the pumpkin mixture into the dry ingredients and mix with a knife until the dough comes together.

Pat the dough out to a thickness of 2 cm on a lightly floured surface and evenly sprinkle on the parmesan, pepitas and pepper. Transfer to the baking tray and, using a lightly floured knife, cut the dough into 9 squares. Bake for 15–20 minutes, until risen and golden. Serve warm.

Makes 9

75 g (½ cup) gluten-free plain flour
160 g (1 cup) brown rice flour
2 teaspoons gluten-free baking powder
50 g (¼ cup) fine polenta (cornmeal)
2 spring onions, thinly sliced
a good pinch of sea salt
250 g pumpkin, steamed and mashed
130 g (½ cup) Greek-style yoghurt
3 tablespoons olive oil
50 g parmesan, very finely grated
1 tablespoon pepitas
cracked black pepper

Pumpkin and fennel soup with black quinoa

Heat the oil in a large saucepan over medium heat, add the fennel and onion and cook for 10 minutes, until the fennel and onion are soft and golden. Stir in the pumpkin, then pour in the stock and cook for 20 minutes, until the soup is thick and creamy. Blend until smooth.

To make the black quinoa topping, rinse the quinoa under cold running water and put into a saucepan. Cover with water, bring to the boil and cook for 25 minutes, until white tails appear; drain. Transfer to a bowl, add the preserved lemon, coriander, dukkah, cinnamon and olive oil and mix to combine.

Serve the pumpkin and fennel soup with the black quinoa topping.

Serves 4

TIP: Take a whole pumpkin in its skin, pop it onto a baking tray and bake in the oven at 180°C until it is really soft, then simply scoop out the flesh.

3 tablespoons olive oil
1 fennel bulb, chopped
1 onion, chopped
500 g roast pumpkin (see Tip)
1 litre (4 cups) chicken or vegetable stock, preferably homemade

Black quinoa topping
50 g (¼ cup) black quinoa, rinsed
1 tablespoon thinly sliced preserved lemon
2 tablespoons chopped coriander leaves
1 teaspoon Hazelnut dukkah (page 103)
½ teaspoon ground cinnamon
1 tablespoon extra virgin olive oil

Adzuki bean and pumpkin stew

Preheat the oven to 200°C.

Put the pumpkin into a roasting tin and roast for 50 minutes, until very soft and golden.

Combine the adzuki beans and 750 ml (3 cups) of water in a very large saucepan, add the kombu and ginger and cook for 1 hour, until the beans are just tender and most of the liquid has evaporated.

Add the pumpkin and tamari to the pan and simmer for 20 minutes, until thick. Season with salt and serve.

Serves 4

½ small kent pumpkin (about 750 g), unpeeled
220 g (1 cup) dried adzuki beans, soaked
   overnight in water, then drained
1 piece of kombu
1 tablespoon finely grated fresh ginger
1 tablespoon tamari
sea salt

One of the most grounding things you can do for yourself is to walk barefoot on dewy morning grass.

Caramelised onion, kale and sweet potato frittata

Preheat the oven to 220°C. Line a baking tray with baking paper.

Place the sweet potato and cherry tomatoes on the prepared tray and roast for 20 minutes. Remove the tomatoes and return the sweet potato to the oven for 15 minutes, until soft and golden.

Meanwhile, heat 2 tablespoons of the oil in a large ovenproof frying pan over medium heat, add the onion and stir occasionally for 15 minutes, until caramelised. Remove from the pan.

Add the remaining oil to the pan to ensure the eggs don't stick. Pour in the eggs, top with the caramelised onion, sweet potato, cherry tomatoes, wilted kale, hummus and olives and cook over medium heat for 5 minutes, until the edge starts to set.

Transfer the pan to the oven and bake for 10 minutes, until the top of the frittata is puffed and golden. Scatter on the lemon thyme and serve.

Serves 4–6

300 g sweet potato, sliced
200 g cherry tomatoes
3 tablespoons olive oil
3 red onions, thinly sliced
8 free-range eggs, lightly beaten
100 g baby kale, wilted
3 tablespoons Herbed hummus (page 62)
50 g (scant ⅓ cup) pitted kalamata olives
6 lemon thyme sprigs

Nori with pumpkin and smoked tofu

Cut the nori sheet into three equal pieces.

Place one nori piece on a work surface and arrange a little of the pumpkin at one end, then top with some tofu, sesame seeds, sprouts and onion. Roll up to enclose the filling and cut into bite-sized pieces. Repeat this process with the remaining ingredients.

Makes about 12

1 nori sheet
200 g roast pumpkin, sliced
100 g smoked tofu, cut into thin strips
1 tablespoon toasted sesame seeds
30 g alfalfa sprouts
2 tablespoons fried onions

dinner

Edamame with chilli and garlic

Cook the edamame in a saucepan of boiling water for 5 minutes, until bright green and tender. Drain well.

Heat the ghee in a frying pan, add the garlic and chilli and cook over medium heat for 2 minutes.

Add the edamame, dried chillies and tamari and toss quickly to coat in the sauce.

Serves 4

250 g frozen shelled edamame
1 tablespoon ghee (page 122)
1 garlic clove, chopped
2 small dried red chillies, torn
1 tablespoon tamari

Steamed vegetables with miso tahini cream

This is my staple dinner. I know that might seem really odd but my job demands I sample a lot of different flavours, so when I am left to choose my favourite meal, I will always pick steamed vegetables. If I am really hungry or have a sweet craving, I might add a cob of corn. If I have a cold, I'll add some cauliflower. In summer I'll squeeze on some lemon juice and drizzle olive oil over. In winter I'll grate on some parmesan and warm up the vegetables with a generous crack of pepper.

Put the carrot, sweet potato and daikon in a single layer in a large steamer, cover with a lid and steam over a saucepan of simmering water for 15–20 minutes, until the vegetables are just soft. Add the broccolini, asparagus and green beans and cook for 5 minutes more, until they are bright green and tender.

To make the miso tahini cream, whisk together the tahini, miso, lime juice, sesame seeds, tamari and sesame oil, then add just enough warm water to thin the dressing until smooth and creamy.

Serve bowls of the steamed vegetables with the dressing drizzled over the top.

Serves 4

2 carrots, cut into thick slices
300 g sweet potato, cut into thick slices
1 daikon radish, cut into thick slices
200 g broccolini, trimmed
6 asparagus spears, woody ends trimmed
200 g green beans, stalks trimmed

Miso tahini cream
3 tablespoons hulled tahini
1 tablespoon shiro miso
1 tablespoon lime juice
1 tablespoon toasted sesame seeds
1 tablespoon tamari
1 teaspoon sesame oil

Chicken and egg donburi

Japanese mothers feed donburi to their children when they are not feeling well. There is something incredibly nourishing about an Asian-style omelette served over rice.

Wash the rice in a sieve until the water runs clear. Put into a saucepan with 500 ml (2 cups) of water and bring to the boil. Cook over high heat until tunnels appear in the rice. Cover with a tight-fitting lid, reduce the heat to as low as possible and cook for 10 minutes, until the water has been absorbed and the rice is tender. Turn off the heat and let the rice sit for 5 minutes, then fluff with a fork to separate the grains. Alternatively, put the rice into a rice cooker, add 2 cups (500 ml) of water and turn the rice cooker on.

Put the stock, tamari and sugar into a large saucepan and stir over low heat until the sugar dissolves. Bring to the boil, without stirring, then reduce the heat to low. Add the chopped chicken and simmer for 5 minutes, until just cooked. Add the spring onion and cook for 1 minute.

Lightly mix the eggs, without beating, and pour into the pan around the chicken in a steady stream, without stirring. Cook for 5 minutes, until the egg around the edge of the pan starts to bubble. Gently stir once, cover and cook for 5 minutes, until the egg is almost set.

Divide the rice between four serving bowls and carefully spoon on a portion of the chicken and egg mixture. Sprinkle with the sesame seeds and extra spring onion.

Serves 4

200 g (1 cup) basmati rice
310 ml (1¼ cups) dashi stock or chicken stock
2 tablespoons tamari
1 tablespoon coconut sugar
300 g free-range chicken thigh fillets, chopped
3 spring onions, sliced, plus extra to garnish
4 free-range eggs
1 tablespoon toasted sesame seeds

Celeriac and parsnip soup

Celeriac is one of those vegetables most people steer clear of because it is a bit of a mystery. Its bulbous quality makes it extremely grounding and when combined with parsnip makes the perfect soup for cold, windy days. The green tea buckwheat soba noodles used here add a lovely flavour and colour and are warming and gentle on the digestive system. If you have trouble finding them, just use buckwheat soba noodles.

Heat the oil and ghee in a large saucepan over medium heat, add the leek and cook, stirring occasionally, for 10 minutes, until soft and golden. Stir in the celeriac and parsnip and cook for 10 minutes, until the vegetables start to soften.

Add the stock and bay leaf to the pan and bring to the boil. Reduce the heat to low and simmer for 40 minutes, until the vegetables are very soft. Remove the bay leaf. Blend the soup until smooth.

Cook the noodles and edamame in a large saucepan of boiling water until tender. Drain and rinse under cold water, then drain well. Add the sesame oil, chilli and onion flakes and toss to combine.

Divide the soup between four serving bowls, top with a mound of noodles and serve.

Serves 4–6

1 tablespoon olive oil
1 tablespoon ghee (page 122)
1 leek, pale part only, washed well and thinly sliced
1 celeriac bulb, peeled and chopped
2 parsnips, peeled and chopped
1.5 litres (6 cups) chicken stock, preferably homemade
1 bay leaf
50 g green tea buckwheat soba noodles
50 g frozen shelled edamame
½ teaspoon sesame oil
pinch of chilli flakes
2 tablespoons fried onion flakes

Kitchari

Soak the rice and split mung beans in cold water for 2 hours, rinse and drain.

Melt the ghee in a large saucepan over medium heat, add the cumin and cook for 1 minute. Stir in the onion, garlic, ginger and turmeric and cook for 5 minutes, until the onion is soft and golden. Add the carrot and zucchini and cook for 5 minutes.

Add the rice, beans and 1.25 litres (5 cups) of water to the pan and bring to the boil. Cook over high heat until tunnels appear in the surface of the rice, reduce the heat to low and simmer for 15 minutes, until the rice and beans are soft and slightly mushy.

Stir in the coriander and lemon juice and season with salt.

Serves 4

200 g (1 cup) basmati rice
225 g (1 cup) split mung beans (moong dal)
2 tablespoons ghee (page 122)
1 teaspoon cumin seeds
1 onion, finely chopped
1 small garlic clove, chopped
½ teaspoon grated fresh ginger
½ teaspoon grated fresh or ¼ teaspoon
   ground turmeric
1 carrot, grated
1 zucchini, grated
1 tablespoon chopped coriander leaves
juice of 1 lemon
pinch of sea salt

Pumpkin and spinach dhal

Put the split mung beans or lentils, ginger, spices, chilli, bay leaf, curry leaves, salt, oil and cherry tomatoes into a large saucepan, add 875 ml (3½ cups) of water and bring to the boil over medium heat. Reduce the heat to low and simmer for 20 minutes, until the beans or lentils are just soft. Don't overcook them, you don't want them to be mushy.

Remove the pan from the heat, stir in 2 teaspoons of the ghee, the lemon juice, pumpkin and spinach, sprinkle with the extra garam masala, cover with a lid and allow to stand for 5 minutes.

Meanwhile, wash the rice in a sieve until the water runs clear. Put the rice in a saucepan with 500 ml (2 cups) of water and the remaining ghee, bring to the boil and cook over high heat until tunnels appear in the rice. Cover with a tight-fitting lid, reduce the heat to as low as possible and cook for 10 minutes, until the water has been absorbed and the rice is tender. Turn off the heat and let the rice sit for 5 minutes, then fluff with a fork.

Serve the dhal with lemon wedges and the basmati rice.

Serves 4

285 g (1¼ cups) split mung beans (moong dal)
   or red lentils
1 tablespoon finely grated fresh ginger
1 teaspoon ground turmeric
1 teaspoon black mustard seeds
1 teaspoon garam masala, plus extra
   for sprinkling
1 small dried red chilli
1 bay leaf
6 curry leaves
1 teaspoon sea salt
½ tablespoon coconut oil
100 g cherry tomatoes, halved
1½ tablespoons ghee (page 122)
1 tablespoon lemon juice
155 g (1 cup) roast chopped pumpkin
100 g baby spinach leaves
200 g (1 cup) basmati rice
lemon wedges, to serve

Ghee

Ghee (clarified butter) is one of the major ingredients in Ayurvedic cooking. It is said to rekindle the digestive fire, making it perfect for anyone with a weak digestive system. Modern science has discovered that ghee contains phenolic antioxidants that support the immune system. When I studied Ayurveda, my gorgeous teacher Dr Ajit used to say if you didn't know what to give someone, just give them ghee. Having said that, people with a Kapha constitution need to use it in moderation.

I use ghee to help calm me down and add a little to warm drinks on cold, windy days. It tastes so yummy in warm milk with cinnamon and cardamom, stirred through warm quinoa porridge or added to rice before you cook it or ... I could go on forever. And just before I finish, know that ghee is the difference between a good and a great dhal.

Melt the butter in a saucepan over low heat. You will notice as it melts that a white foam settles on the surface – these are the milk solids. When I am being finicky, I like to skim this foam off using a spoon, but if I am in a rush, I leave it and strain it out at the end.

Continue cooking the butter until the shape of the bubbles on top changes and then stops altogether; this usually takes about 5–10 minutes. The ghee will smell nutty and when you tilt the pan you will see the milk solids on the base have turned golden brown, giving the ghee a wonderful flavour.

Allow the melted butter to cool slightly for a couple of minutes. Line a stainless steel sieve with paper towel or an unused Chux cloth and place over a bowl. Strain the melted butter into the bowl. You will be left with clarified butter – better known as ghee. Store in a sterilised glass jar or metal tin. The ghee will solidify as it cools.

Use ghee in any place you would use butter or oil. It withstands higher temperatures than butter because the clarifying process removes all the impurities.

Makes about 200 g

250 g organic unsalted butter

Indian vegetable and cashew curry

I find a curry is always better the next day or made a few hours ahead of time and allowed to rest. In winter, I lean towards tomato-based curries and in summer, coconut-based curries. If I have time, I roast my spices, then grind each one separately – it makes a world of difference to the flavour of the dish. I accompany my winter curry with a spicy mango chutney and eggplant pickle.

Heat the ghee in a large saucepan over medium heat, add the onion and cook, stirring occasionally, for 10 minutes, until soft and golden. Add the spices and cook until fragrant. Stir in the vegetables, cashews, tomatoes and 250 ml (1 cup) of water, turn the heat to low, cover and simmer for 20 minutes. Remove the lid and simmer for 15 minutes, until the vegetables are soft.

Remove from the heat and stir the yoghurt into the curry. Sprinkle on the extra cashews and serve with the brown rice.

Serves 4–6

2 tablespoons ghee (page 122)
1 red onion, finely chopped
1 teaspoon ground cumin
1 teaspoon ground coriander
1 teaspoon turmeric
½ teaspoon chilli powder
1 teaspoon garam masala
6 fresh curry leaves
1 carrot, thickly sliced
300 g pumpkin, cut into cubes
2 zucchini, sliced
1 red capsicum, chopped
200 g cauliflower, cut into florets
40 g (¼ cup) raw cashews, plus extra to serve
400 g can chopped tomatoes
130 g (½ cup) plain yoghurt
steamed brown rice, to serve

Steamed greens with nori and spiced almond salt

I eat this as a meal, but you can serve these vegetables as an accompaniment, too. This recipe makes more of the spiced almond salt than you will need for one serve of vegetables. Store leftovers in an airtight jar for up to 2 weeks.

Place the Asian greens, broccolini, snow peas and edamame in a steamer basket over a saucepan of simmering water, cover and steam for 5 minutes, until bright green and tender.

Pound half of the nori, the almonds, linseeds, salt, chilli flakes and five-spice in a mortar and pestle to form a crunchy salt.

Sprinkle the spiced salt over the greens. Finish by sprinkling on the rest of the nori, the white pepper and a dollop of ghee.

Serves 2 as a meal or 4 as a side

1 bunch of bok choy, trimmed
1 bunch of Chinese broccoli (gai larn), trimmed
1 bunch of broccolini, trimmed
200 g snow peas
60 g (1 cup) frozen shelled edamame
1 nori sheet, cut into thin strips
40 g (¼ cup) chopped blanched almonds
2 tablespoons linseeds (flaxseeds)
1 teaspoon sea salt
¼ teaspoon chilli flakes
½ teaspoon Chinese five-spice
cracked white pepper
ghee (page 122), to serve

treats

Yummy in my tummy black rice pudding

Adzuki beans are highly prized by the Japanese and Chinese, believed to help reduce sugar cravings. They strengthen and support the spleen and are the most easily digested of all the beans. Black rice is said to support and nourish the kidneys. The spices I've used here help warm the coconut milk. Turmeric is a wonder spice. It is anti-inflammatory, antibacterial and antifungal.

Put the rice and adzuki beans in separate bowls, cover with cold water and leave to soak overnight.

Drain the rice and combine with 1 litre (4 cups) of cold water in a saucepan. Bring to the boil, then reduce the heat to low and simmer for 20–30 minutes, until tender. Drain.

Drain the beans and transfer to a saucepan, cover with plenty of water and simmer for 40 minutes, until just soft. Drain.

Combine the coconut milk, coconut sugar and spices in a saucepan over medium heat and stir until the sugar dissolves. Add the beans and rice and cook for 10 minutes, until thick, creamy and heated through. Drizzle the extra coconut milk over the top and sprinkle with a little extra cinnamon.

Serves 4–6

200 g (1 cup) black glutinous rice
55 g (¼ cup) adzuki beans
125 ml (½ cup) coconut milk, plus extra to serve
2 tablespoons coconut sugar
½ teaspoon ground cinnamon, plus extra to serve
½ teaspoon ground cardamom
½ teaspoon ground ginger
pinch of turmeric

Chamomile and orange blossom poached pears

Put the flowers, orange blossom water, spices and 2 cups (500 ml) of water into a saucepan. Stir in the sugar and continue to stir over low heat until it dissolves.

Add the whole pears to the pan and simmer over medium heat for 15–20 minutes, until the fruit is tender.

Serves 4

2 tablespoons dried chamomile flowers
1 tablespoon orange blossom water
1 cinnamon stick
4 whole cloves
3 tablespoons coconut sugar
4 ripe pears, peeled

Pumpkin cheesecake with sesame peanut crunch

At the beginning of every week in autumn and winter I bake a whole pumpkin. I don't do anything to it, just leave it in its skin and pop it onto a baking tray and bake it until it is really soft. I then have the basis for my meals for the week. I will make pumpkin soup, pumpkin tart and then a sweet treat of some sort. So when I say pumpkin puree, I really just mean soft, roast pumpkin flesh, scooped from its skin.

Preheat the oven to 180°C. Grease and line the base of a 20 cm springform cake tin with baking paper and wrap the outside of the tin in a few sheets of foil. Place some water in a baking dish that is large enough to hold the cake tin and transfer to the oven to heat.

Put the pumpkin puree, quark or cream cheese and sugar into a food processor and process until smooth. Add the eggs, egg yolks and spices and process until combined.

Pour the pumpkin mixture into the prepared tin, then place in the preheated baking dish and bake for 30 minutes, until just set. Turn off the oven and allow to cool in the oven with the door ajar.

To make the sesame peanut crunch, combine the sesame seeds and peanuts in a frying pan and toast, shaking the pan every now and then so they don't burn, over medium heat for 5 minutes, until the nuts are golden brown. Transfer to a mortar and pestle, add the sugar and pound until the nuts are coarsely crushed and the seeds have burst.

To serve, remove the pumpkin cheesecake from the tin, sprinkle with the sesame peanut crunch and cut into wedges.

Serves 8

250 g pumpkin puree
450 g quark or good-quality cream cheese
65 g ($\frac{1}{3}$ cup) coconut sugar
2 free-range eggs
2 free-range egg yolks
1 tablespoon finely grated fresh ginger
1 teaspoon ground cinnamon
½ teaspoon ground cloves

Sesame peanut crunch
1 tablespoon black sesame seeds
3 tablespoons unsalted peanuts
1 tablespoon coconut sugar

Black sesame chocolate cake

This is my favourite cake ever, ever, ever. Black sesame seeds are the bomb. In Ayurveda we use them to warm and settle nervous energy. I rub cold-pressed, not toasted, sesame oil into my body to help ground and warm me, and I eat as much black sesame as I can. If I have an upset stomach, I rub the warmed oil around my navel in a clockwise direction; it always makes me feel better.

Preheat the oven to 180°C. Grease and line a 20 cm square cake tin.

Put the sesame seeds into a mortar and pestle or spice mill and grind to a smooth paste.

Put the butter and sesame paste into a saucepan and cook over low heat until the butter melts. Remove from the heat and stir in the eggs and sugar.

Combine the almond meal, flour and baking powder in a bowl, then sift over the egg mixture and gently fold to combine. Pour into the prepared tin and bake for 35–40 minutes, until a skewer inserted in the centre comes out clean. Allow the cake to stand in the tin for 10 minutes before turning out onto a wire rack to cool completely.

To make the chocolate ganache, combine the chocolate and cream in a saucepan over low heat and cook, stirring occasionally, until the chocolate melts. Remove from the heat and allow to cool for 15 minutes, until thickened.

Spread the chocolate ganache over the cake and allow to set. Cut into small pieces to serve.

Serves 8–10

200 g (1⅓ cups) black sesame seeds
200 g butter, chopped
3 free-range eggs, lightly beaten
185 g (1 cup) coconut sugar
100 g (1 cup) almond meal
35 g (¼ cup) gluten-free plain flour
1 teaspoon gluten-free baking powder

Chocolate ganache
200 g dark chocolate, chopped
100 ml pure cream

Rubbing warm, cold-pressed sesame oil on your feet before you go to bed will help you rest peacefully.

Steamed vanilla and green tea custards

I use unhomogenised organic cow's milk in all my cooking. I only ever have it warmed, not cold, as it is harder to digest and more mucus-forming when it is chilled. If you have a milk allergy, you can use the milk of your choice in any of these recipes, but remember that rice and soy milk tend to be sweet and cooling, and nut milks are more heating.

Whisk together the eggs, vanilla, milk, tea or acai powder and maple syrup, then strain into a jug.

Divide the mixture between four heatproof tea cups. Place in a large bamboo steamer, cover with a lid and steam over a saucepan of simmering water, ensuring the water doesn't touch the base of the steamer, for 10 minutes, until the custard is just set. Do not overcook or the custard will be watery.

To serve, invert the custards and sprinkle with extra green tea or acai powder.

Serves 4

4 free-range eggs, lightly beaten
1 teaspoon natural vanilla extract
2 cups (500 ml) unhomogenised organic milk
1 tablespoon matcha green tea powder
    or acai powder, plus extra to sprinkle
2 tablespoons pure maple syrup

Creamed rice with baked baby pears

Preheat the oven to 180°C.

Put the pear halves, cut side down, into a baking dish, dot with the ghee, sprinkle on the saffron and pour on the pear juice. Cover the dish with foil and bake for 20 minutes. Remove the foil and bake, turning once, for 20 minutes more, until the pears are soft and caramelised and the liquid is thick and sticky.

Meanwhile, put the rice, milk and vanilla bean into a saucepan and cook, stirring regularly, over medium heat for 30 minutes, until the rice is soft and the mixture is thick and creamy.

Serve the creamed rice with the sticky baked pears and their juice.

Serves 4

8 baby pears, halved
1 tablespoon ghee (page 122)
pinch of saffron threads
250 ml (1 cup) unsweetened pear juice
90 g (½ cup) arborio rice
1 litre (4 cups) unhomogenised organic milk
1 vanilla bean, split lengthways

Chrysanthemum and licorice tea

This drink is good for grounding or bringing down the temperature in the body. It is recommended for treating fever, swollen glands or headaches. It is not recommended when you are pregnant. Licorice is naturally sweet, so I find I don't need any extra sweetener.

Put the chrysanthemum flowers and licorice into a teapot, top with 500 ml (2 cups) of boiling water, and allow to steep for 5 minutes.

Drink hot or chilled.

Serves 4

TIP: Chrysanthemum flowers and licorice root can be purchased at health food stores.

2 tablespoons dried chrysanthemum flowers (see Tip)
1 teaspoon licorice root (see Tip)

Pear and pumpkin spiced loaf

Preheat the oven to 180°C. Grease and line an 8 cm x 22 cm loaf tin with baking paper.

Sift the flour, baking powder, bicarbonate of soda and spices into a bowl, then stir in the almond meal.

Beat the coconut oil and sugar in a bowl until light and creamy. Add the egg and pear and beat until combined. Fold in the dry ingredients, then the pumpkin and yoghurt.

Spoon the mixture into the prepared tin and bake for 40 minutes, until a skewer inserted in the centre comes out clean.

Serves 6–8

150 g (1 cup) gluten-free plain flour
1 teaspoon gluten-free baking powder
1 teaspoon bicarbonate of soda
1 teaspoon ground cinnamon
1 teaspoon freshly grated nutmeg
1 teaspoon ground ginger
50 g (½ cup) almond meal
125 ml (½ cup) coconut oil
90 g (½ cup) coconut sugar
1 free-range egg
2 very ripe pears, grated
60 g (½ cup) grated pumpkin
260 g (1 cup) Greek-style yoghurt

Spiced nut butter cookies

These totally delicious, melt-in-your-mouth cookies are fragile and a little crumbly. You can use gluten-free flour instead of the buckwheat and rice flours but these are more warming.

Preheat the oven to 180°C. Line a baking tray with baking paper.

Mix the chia seeds with 3 tablespoons of water and set aside for 10 minutes.

Beat the coconut oil and sugar in a bowl until light and creamy. Add the super spread or nut butter, vanilla and chia seed mixture and beat until smooth. Fold in the flours, cinnamon and nuts.

Spoon tablespoons of the cookie mixture onto the prepared tray, allowing for spreading. Bake for 20 minutes, until golden brown.

Allow to cool on the tray.

Makes 12

1 tablespoon white chia seeds
125 ml (½ cup) coconut oil
90 g (½ cup) coconut sugar
125 g (½ cup) super spread or nut butter
2 teaspoons natural vanilla extract
130 g (1 cup) buckwheat flour
155 g (1 cup) brown rice flour
1 teaspoon ground cinnamon
50 g (⅓ cup) walnuts or whole almonds

A cup of this and a cup of that cake

Preheat the oven to 180°C. Grease and line an 8 cm x 22 cm loaf tin with baking paper.

Put the coconut, flour, baking powder, walnuts and sugar into a bowl. Stir in the mashed banana and almond milk and mix to combine. Pour into the prepared tin and bake for 40 minutes, until a skewer inserted in the centre comes out clean.

Allow to cool in the tin on a wire rack before turning out.

Serves 6–8

90 g (1 cup) desiccated coconut
150 g (1 cup) gluten-free plain flour
2 teaspoons gluten-free baking powder
170 g (1 cup) walnuts
185 g (1 cup) coconut sugar
240 g (1 cup) mashed banana (about 3 large ripe bananas)
250 ml (1 cup) unsweetened almond milk

FOODS THAT WARM
for cold days

AMARANTH, BASIL, BAY LEAVES, BEETROOT, BUCKWHEAT, CAPSICUM, CARDAMOM, CARROTS, CHIA SEEDS, CHILLI, CINNAMON, CLOVES, CORN, DAIKON RADISH, EGGPLANT, EGGS, FENUGREEK, GARAM MASALA, GARLIC, GINGER, KIDNEY BEANS, LENTILS, LINSEEDS (FLAXSEEDS), MANGO, MILLET, MISO, MUSHROOMS, MUSTARD, NUTS, OLIVES, ORANGE ZEST, OREGANO, PAPAYA , PARSLEY, POLENTA, POPPY SEEDS, PUMPKIN, QUINOA, RADISH, SALT, SEAWEED, SESAME SEEDS, STAR ANISE, TEMPEH, TOMATOES, WATERCRESS, YOGHURT, AMARANTH, BASIL, BAY LEAVES, BEETROOT, BUCKWHEAT, CAPSICUM, CARDAMOM, CARROTS, CHIA SEEDS, CHILLI, CINNAMON, CLOVES, CORN...

breakfast

Smoked salmon kedgeree

Break the salmon into large pieces.

Heat the ghee in a large non-stick frying pan, add the spring onion and spices and cook over medium heat until the mustard seeds start to pop.

Add the salmon, millet, corn and 1 litre (4 cups) of water to the pan and bring to the boil. Reduce the heat to low, cover and cook for 25 minutes, until the millet is soft and the corn is tender. Add the eggs and parsley and cook for 5 minutes. Remove from the heat and season with the lemon zest and juice.

Serves 4

300 g hot-smoked salmon
2 tablespoons ghee (page 122)
3 spring onions, sliced
1 tablespoon grated fresh ginger
1 teaspoon garam masala
1 teaspoon curry powder
1 teaspoon black mustard seeds
210 g (1 cup) millet, rinsed
200 g (1 cup) corn kernels
2 hard-boiled free-range eggs,
    peeled and quartered
2 tablespoons chopped flat-leaf parsley leaves
finely grated zest and juice of 1 lemon

Ginger tea

Anyone who knows me knows I am the queen of ginger tea in winter. If you visit me, that is what you are offered. I usually don't strain it, just slice a few pieces, add them to my cup and pour in the hot water. It is my medicine. If I am going to be at home all day, then I will pop a big pan of it on and let it simmer until I have a big gingery brew. I then use this is in everything. I could bang on forever about the goodness of ginger. In short, ginger is great for digestion and nausea, has anti-inflammatory properties and relieves colds and flus. Best of all, it tastes amazing.

Put the ginger into cups, pour over 500 ml (2 cups) of boiling water and allow to brew for a few minutes before drinking. Make sure you chew on the little ginger shreds in the bottom of your cup, they are really yummy.

Serves 2–4

2 tablespoons finely shredded fresh ginger

Warm your toes winter chai

The fussiest chai drinker in the world, I rarely order it when I'm out because it's never spicy enough and I have been spoilt by too many incredibly delicious masala chais in India. The secret to a great brew is time. The longer you allow the spices to bathe in the liquid, the richer, spicier and more divinely aromatic your chai will be. I don't use black tea in my chai because I prefer it without but I have given the option of it here for those who like a caffeine hit.

Crush each spice separately in a mortar and pestle, then transfer to a large saucepan. Add 1 litre (4 cups) of water and bring to the boil over high heat. Reduce the heat to low and simmer for 20 minutes, until the mixture is deep brown and fragrant. This is where the rich spice flavour comes from, so you don't want to rush this process or your chai will taste weak and watery.

Add the tea, if using, and milk to the pan and cook over low heat for 15 minutes more. Strain and sweeten with the sugar, if desired.

Serves 4

6 cardamom pods
6 whole cloves
1 cinnamon stick
3 black peppercorns
3 star anise
a thumb-sized piece of ginger, sliced
2 teaspoons black tea leaves or
  1 black tea bag (optional)
250 ml (1 cup) unhomogenised organic milk
dark palm sugar, to taste (optional)

Feta and tomato polenta porridge

Combine 750 ml (3 cups) of water, the tomatoes and bay leaf in a saucepan, place over high heat and bring to the boil. Slowly pour in the polenta, whisking constantly to stop it from becoming lumpy. Change to a wooden spoon and continue to stir until the polenta is thick and starts to come away from the side of the pan. Gently stir in the basil and feta. Remove from the heat and cover while you cook the spinach.

Heat the oil in a large frying pan, add the garlic and seeds and cook over medium heat for 1 minute, until the garlic starts to colour. Add the spinach and cook for 3 minutes, just until the spinach wilts.

Fold the spinach through the polenta and serve immediately. The polenta will thicken on standing.

Serves 4

100 g cherry tomatoes, halved
1 bay leaf
170 g (1 cup) fine polenta (cornmeal)
a handful of basil leaves
100 g marinated goat's feta
1 tablespoon olive oil
1 garlic clove, thinly sliced
1 tablespoon pepitas
1 tablespoon linseeds (flaxseeds)
150 g baby spinach

Spicy sunshine egg

Combine the flours, salt, spinach, chilli and nigella seeds in a bowl, then stir in the oil and 250 ml (1 cup) of warm water and continue to stir until the batter is smooth.

Heat 1 teaspoon of the ghee in a large non-stick frying pan, add 3 tablespoons of batter to the pan and cook over medium heat until small bubbles appear on the surface. Crack one egg into the centre of the chapatti, then fold the chapatti over the egg.

Cover the pan and cook for 3 minutes, until the egg is cooked to your liking. Repeat with the remaining ghee, batter and eggs.

Serve each chapati and egg drizzled with the chilli sauce or kasoundi and topped with the fried onions.

Serves 4 (2 chapatis each)

85 g (½ cup) brown rice flour
65 g (½ cup) chickpea flour (besan)
pinch of sea salt
55 g (1 cup) finely shredded English spinach
1 long green chilli, seeded and chopped
1 teaspoon nigella seeds
2 tablespoons olive oil
1 tablespoon ghee (page 122)
8 free-range eggs
sriracha chilli sauce or Kasoundi (page 102), to serve
sunflower sprouts, to serve
fried onions, to serve

Toasted buckwheat, chia and millet granola

This isn't granola in the true sense of the word. I've used warming buckwheat and millet instead of oats.

Preheat the oven to 160°C. Line two baking trays with baking paper. Put the buckwheat, millet, chia seeds, spices and seeds in a bowl and mix to combine.

Combine the nut butter, ghee and rice syrup in a saucepan and stir over low heat until the nut butter softens and the mixture is smooth. Add to the buckwheat mixture and mix well.

Spread the mixture on the prepared trays, bake for 10 minutes, turn and bake the other side for a further 10 minutes, until crisp and golden. Stir in the raisins and goji berries.

Allow the granola to cool on the trays, then break into bite-sized pieces. Serve with the warm milk.

Makes 500 g (4 cups)

190 g (1 cup) buckwheat
95 g (½ cup) millet
75 g (½ cup) white chia seeds
1 teaspoon ground ginger
1 teaspoon ground cinnamon
1 teaspoon ground cardamom
½ teaspoon ground cloves
3 tablespoons linseeds (flaxseeds)
3 tablespoons pepitas
2 tablespoons sesame seeds
3 tablespoons nut butter
3 tablespoons ghee (page 122)
3 tablespoons brown rice syrup
3 tablespoons raisins
3 tablespoons goji berries
milk of your choice, warmed, to serve

Orange-spiced quinoa porridge with honey pepper yoghurt

In the cooler months I like to warm up my yoghurt with some ginger or pepper, especially if I am sweetening it. (Remember, sweet is cooling.) I know honey pepper yoghurt may sound a touch odd, but it is really very tasty.

Put the quinoa and chia seeds in a saucepan, add 500 ml (2 cups) of water, the orange zest, spices and salt and cook, stirring constantly, over medium heat for 5 minutes, until the quinoa is thick and creamy. Stir in the milk and ghee and cook until the porridge is heated through.

To make the honey pepper yoghurt, fold together the honey, peppercorns and yoghurt.

Serve the porridge with the honey pepper yoghurt on top. Finish with the raisins and almonds and extra orange slices and zest.

Serves 4

95 g (1 cup) quinoa flakes
1 teaspoon white chia seeds
finely grated zest of 1 orange, plus extra to serve
1 teaspoon ground cinnamon
1 teaspoon ground ginger
½ teaspoon ground cardamom
pinch of sea salt
250 ml (1 cup) unhomogenised organic milk
    or unsweetened almond milk
1 teaspoon ghee (page 122)
2 tablespoons raisins
2 tablespoons whole almonds, soaked
    overnight and sliced
orange slices, to serve

Honey pepper yoghurt
1 teaspoon raw honey
½ teaspoon cracked pink peppercorns
4 tablespoons Greek-style yoghurt

Flu fighter tea

You will notice that I add the honey last when the tea is warm rather than hot. This is because in Ayurveda, heating honey above 40°C is a big no-no, which is why I tend to cook with pure maple syrup and coconut sugar and never honey. This is also the reason I recommend raw honey rather than store-bought honey, as heating honey destroys a lot of its medicinal properties.

Put the fenugreek, ginger, turmeric and lemon juice into a teapot, add 1 litre (4 cups) of boiling water and allow to steep and cool for 15 minutes.

Stir in the honey. Strain into cups and serve.

Serves 2–4

1 teaspoon fenugreek seeds
a thumb-sized piece of fresh ginger, thinly sliced
1 teaspoon sliced fresh turmeric
1 tablespoon lemon juice
1 teaspoon raw honey

Honey is considered different to all other sweeteners in Ayurveda. It is warming, whereas other sweeteners like maple syrup and sugar are cooling. It is thought that eating locally produced honey can help protect against asthma and hayfever.

Shakshuka

I got to know shakshuka when I was living in Jerusalem in my 20s. Here I have used haloumi but you could use marinated feta. The sauce always tastes better the next day.

Heat the oil in a large frying pan, add the onion, chilli and capsicum and cook over medium heat for 10 minutes, until the onion is soft and golden. Add the paprika and cinnamon and cook for 1 minute, until fragrant.

Add the tomatoes and haloumi to the pan and cook for 10 minutes, until the tomatoes are soft and pulpy. Stir in the spinach, oregano and 3 tablespoons of water and cook for 3 minutes, until the spinach wilts.

Make four small indentations in the top of the sauce with the back of a spoon, leaving a bit of space between each one. Crack the eggs into the holes, cover the pan and cook for 3 minutes, until the whites are cooked but the yolks are soft.

Top the mixture with spoonfuls of the yoghurt and sprinkle on the watercress. Serve with the warm corn tortillas, if using.

Serves 4

1 tablespoon olive oil
1 red onion, finely chopped
1 long red chilli, finely chopped
200 g chargrilled red capsicum from a jar, cut into thin strips
1 teaspoon sweet smoked paprika
1 teaspoon ground cinnamon
400 g can chopped tomatoes
100 g haloumi, chopped
100 g baby spinach
2 tablespoons chopped oregano leaves
4 free-range eggs
Greek-style yoghurt, to serve
watercress, to serve
8 white corn tortillas, warmed (optional)

Eggs for any time

Put the eggs, lentils, basil, capers, feta and tomato in a bowl and mix gently to combine.

Toast the bread until golden and serve the egg mixture on top.

Serves 2–4

3 hard-boiled free-range eggs, chopped
55 g (1 cup) cooked puy lentils
1 tablespoon finely shredded basil leaves
1 teaspoon baby capers, rinsed
50 g goat's feta
2 small vine-ripened tomatoes, finely chopped
4 slices of rice and chia bread

lunch

Warm haloumi, lentil and eggplant salad

Haloumi is heating, so use it in moderation, especially if you are a fiery, competitive Pitta type who, like me, is attracted to those salty, more intensely flavoured cheeses.

I need to talk about cooking eggplant here. If you are frying eggplant, you need to use quite a bit of oil. The eggplant absorbs the oil, but as it cools, it releases the oil, so make sure you drain it on paper towel before serving it.

Preheat the oven to 200°C. Line a baking tray with baking paper.

Put the lentils into a saucepan, cover with water and cook over medium heat for 20 minutes, until just soft. Be careful not to overcook them or they will break up when you mix the salad. Drain and set aside.

Heat the oil in a large frying pan, add the eggplant, in batches, and cook over medium heat until golden brown. Transfer the eggplant to the prepared tray, add the capsicum and onion and bake for 30 minutes, until the vegetables are tender.

Cook the haloumi, without oil, in a non-stick frying pan over medium heat until golden brown on both sides.

Put the lentils, vegetables, parsley and haloumi into a bowl.

To make the dressing, whisk together the mustard, garlic, orange juice and olive oil.

Pour the dressing over the salad and gently mix to combine.

Serves 4–6

210 g (1 cup) puy lentils
3 tablespoons olive oil
4 small eggplants, halved
1 red capsicum, cut into thick strips
2 red onions, cut into wedges
400 g haloumi, thickly sliced
a handful of flat-leaf parsley leaves, chopped

Dressing
1 tablespoon dijon mustard
1 garlic clove, crushed
1 tablespoon orange juice
2 tablespoons olive oil

Millet and vegetable patties with harissa yoghurt

In case you haven't noticed, I have a bit of a thing for millet. I like that it can be cooked in a rice cooker, it tastes and looks similar to couscous and at the time of writing this book is about one-quarter of the price of quinoa. It is a good source of magnesium and fibre and was the staple grain in Europe before potatoes and corn were introduced. Millet takes about 25 minutes to cook and requires double the amount of liquid to the grain.

Preheat the oven to 200°C. Line a baking tray with baking paper.

Put the millet into a saucepan, cover with 500 ml (2 cups) of water and bring to the boil. Reduce the heat to low, cover with a lid and cook for 25 minutes, until the millet is tender and the liquid has been absorbed. Alternatively, put the millet into a rice cooker with 500 ml (2 cups) of water and cook until soft.

Combine the chickpeas, parsley, tahini and curry powder in a food processor, process until smooth. Transfer to a bowl and fold in the millet, egg and vegetables. Using wet hands, shape the mixture into patties, then press into the combined chia and sesame seeds.

Place on the prepared tray and bake for 30 minutes, until crisp and golden.

Put the yoghurt and harissa in a bowl and gently fold together.

Serve the patties with the harissa yoghurt and the pickled vegetables.

Serves 4

210 g (1 cup) millet, rinsed
400 g can chickpeas, rinsed and drained
a handful of flat-leaf parsley leaves, coarsely chopped
1 tablespoon hulled tahini
2 teaspoons curry powder
1 free-range egg, lightly whisked
1 small onion, grated
1 carrot, grated
1 zucchini, grated
125 g (1 cup) grated pumpkin
1 tablespoon black chia seeds
2 tablespoons sesame seeds
130 g (½ cup) Greek-style yoghurt
½ teaspoon harissa
Pickled vegetables (page 164), to serve

Nourishing chicken soup

This is the favourite recipe ever of my friend Kelly, who is also the wonderful designer of this book. I first made it for her a couple of years ago when she was poorly. She hasn't stopped mentioning it since. You should have seen her joy when I sent her home with the whole pot after we photographed it for these pages.

Simmer your soup until the meat falls away from the bones, topping up the water as needed. I never bother removing all the bones, just the big ones my tongs can find. I like to chew on the smaller ones because the marrow inside them is also very healing.

Put the chicken into a very large saucepan or stockpot, add the spices, spring onion, garlic, ginger, celery, carrot, shaoxing rice wine and 4 litres (16 cups) of water and cook over medium heat for 3 hours, until the chicken is very soft and falling away from the bones. You may need to add more water during this time to keep the chicken covered. Remove any large bones and discard.

Add the tamari, cauliflower and corn kernels to the soup and cook for 15 minutes, until the cauliflower is soft. Add the broccoli and cook for 5 minutes, until soft.

Serves 6–8

1 x 1.6 kg free-range chicken
1 cinnamon stick
3 star anise
4 whole cloves
6 black peppercorns
2 tablespoons coriander roots
6 spring onions
1 garlic bulb, halved
5 cm piece of fresh ginger, sliced
3 celery stalks, chopped
3 carrots, chopped
250 ml (1 cup) shaoxing rice wine (optional)
1 tablespoon tamari
300 g cauliflower, cut into florets
2 cobs corn, kernels removed
300 g broccoli, cut into florets

I wholeheartedly believe that chicken soup is medicine. There is magic in this broth; it nourishes as no other food can, calms the body and soothes the worried mind.

Corn with salt and pepper seeds

I find corn is very filling and often have it for lunch or dinner. And I try to have seeds with most of my meals – they are a simple way of adding protein, which helps fill me up, and are packed with goodness.

Put the corn cobs into a large saucepan of water and cook over high heat for 15 minutes, until the corn is tender. Drain well.

Meanwhile, toast the white and pink peppercorns in a frying pan over medium heat for 3 minutes, until fragrant. Add the salt and seeds and cook, giving the pan a shake occasionally, for another 3 minutes. Transfer the mixture to a mortar and pestle and pound to form a coarse salt.

Brush the corn cobs with the ghee and sprinkle with the salt and pepper seeds.

Serves 4

4 corn cobs
½ teaspoon white peppercorns
1 teaspoon pink peppercorns
½ teaspoon pink sea salt
2 tablespoons sunflower seeds
3 tablespoons ghee (page 122)

Pickled vegetables

If you haven't already heard, fermented foods are the new thing – but there is nothing new about them. Just about every culture has eaten fermented foods since the beginning of time. It is not just a great way of preserving food, it also helps us maintain the healthy bacteria in our gut.

Preheat the oven to 100°C. Wash a 500 ml (2 cup) glass preserving jar in hot, soapy water, then rinse. Place the jar upside down on a baking tray and transfer to the oven to dry. After 10 minutes, invert and continue to heat until the jar is completely dry.

Layer the vegetables and spices in your sterilised jar.

Whisk the vinegar, 125 ml (½ cup) of water, the sugar and salt in a bowl until the sugar dissolves. Pour over the vegetables.

Seal the jar and allow to stand overnight or longer if you want them to be more pickled. The longer they are left, the tastier they will be. I usually leave them for a week or two before I use them.

Makes 520 g (2 cups)

75 g (1 cup) shredded Chinese cabbage (wong bok)
1 Lebanese cucumber, thinly sliced
1 teaspoon coriander seeds
1 teaspoon fennels seeds
1 teaspoon black peppercorns
1 small red chilli
1 carrot, thinly sliced
50 g sunflower sprouts
1 small daikon radish or 6 red radishes, thinly sliced
1 small red onion, thinly sliced
1 tablespoon sliced fresh ginger
1 cinnamon stick
250 ml (1 cup) rice wine vinegar
2 teaspoons coconut sugar
2 teaspoons sea salt

Speckled quinoa sushi

Put the quinoa in a saucepan of water and bring to the boil over high heat. Reduce the heat and simmer for 15 minutes, until tails appear and separate from the grain. Rinse under cold water and drain well to remove any excess moisture. Stir in the rice vinegar and allow to cool completely.

Lay a sheet of nori on a bamboo sushi mat, place 2 tablespoons of cooked quinoa at one end, flatten slightly, then top with some tofu, capsicum, cucumber and pickled ginger, allowing a little capsicum, cucumber and tofu to overhang the top edge of the nori. Roll up into a cone and seal the end with a few grains of quinoa. Repeat with the remaining nori sheets. Serve with small bowls of the tamari and wasabi.

Serves 4

100 g (½ cup) tricoloured quinoa, rinsed
2 teaspoons seasoned rice vinegar
4 nori sheets
150 g smoked tofu
1 red capsicum, thinly sliced
1 small Lebanese cucumber, cut into thin strips
1 tablespoon undyed pickled ginger
tamari, to serve
wasabi, to serve

Nori omelette with miso mushroom broth

This recipe is a great way to start your day. I find if I have eggs for breakfast, I am not hungry or distracted by food until lunchtime. If you don't have dashi, you could use a homemade stock. I use red miso in winter and lighter shiro miso in the hotter months as it is less salty.

Whisk together the eggs and spring onion.

Heat ½ tablespoon of the oil in a 20 cm non-stick frying pan over medium heat. Add a quarter of the eggs and top with a quarter of the torn nori. Cook until the edge starts to set, then lift the edge and tilt the pan so that any uncooked egg runs underneath. Cook until just set, then turn over and cook on the other side until set. Transfer to a plate and keep warm. Repeat to make four omelettes in total.

Heat the remaining oil in a large non-stick frying pan over high heat, add the mushrooms and cook for 5 minutes, until they are golden brown and any moisture has evaporated.

Blend the miso with the dashi, pour over the mushrooms, reduce the heat to low and cook, without boiling, for 5 minutes.

Place each omelette in a shallow bowl and pour over the miso mushroom broth. Top with the extra nori and spring onion.

Serves 4

8 free-range eggs
4 spring onions, sliced, plus extra to serve
3 tablespoons olive oil
2 nori sheets, torn, plus extra to serve
300 g mixed mushrooms (such as shiitake, enoki, Swiss brown, chestnut, oyster)
1 teaspoon red miso
250 ml (1 cup) hot dashi stock

In winter, I wrap warmed cooking salt in a tea towel and lay it over my kidneys; it warms me to the bones.

Nourishing buckwheat risotto

Toast the buckwheat in a large frying pan over medium heat for 10 minutes, until it smells toasted and nutty. Set aside.

Heat the oil in a large saucepan over medium heat, add the onion and cook, stirring occasionally, for 10 minutes, until golden. Stir in the celery, carrot and capsicum and cook for 5 minutes, until starting to soften. Sprinkle the paprika over the vegetables and cook, stirring, for 1 minute, until fragrant.

Add the buckwheat, tomatoes, orange zest, bay leaves and stock to the pan and bring to the boil. Reduce the heat to low and simmer for 40 minutes, until the buckwheat grains are tender. You may need to add some hot water if the buckwheat starts to dry out.

Just before serving, stir in the spinach and cook until wilted. Serve the risotto topped with the haloumi and sprinkled with the pepitas.

Serves 4

245 g (1¼ cups) buckwheat, rinsed
2 tablespoons olive oil
1 onion, chopped
2 celery stalks, chopped
1 carrot, chopped
1 red capsicum, chopped
1 teaspoon hot smoked paprika
400 g can chopped tomatoes
finely grated zest of 1 orange
2 bay leaves
750 ml (3 cups) vegetable stock
150 g baby spinach leaves, finely shredded
100 g haloumi, grated
2 tablespoons pepitas

Steamed eggplant with black vinegar dressing

Cut the eggplants in half lengthways and sprinkle with salt. Set aside for 5 minutes. Rinse and pat dry with paper towel.

Place the eggplant in a shallow heatproof bowl and transfer to a bamboo steamer over a saucepan of simmering water. Cover and cook for 10 minutes, until the eggplant is soft. Drain off any excess liquid.

Whisk together the garlic, ginger, chilli, sesame oil, vinegar and sugar and pour over the eggplant. Top with the basil and paprika.

Serves 4

4 Japanese eggplants
2 garlic cloves, finely chopped
1 tablespoon finely shredded fresh ginger
1 long red chilli, seeded and thinly sliced
½ teaspoon sesame oil
3 tablespoons black vinegar
1 teaspoon coconut sugar
Thai basil sprigs, to serve
hot paprika, to serve

Tandoori cauliflower and tempeh

I have to be honest, I have struggled with tempeh in the past. I found the flavour overpowering when I cooked it in stir-fries or on the barbecue. I don't know if it was because I was purchasing inferior quality supermarket tempeh or if I just had not found the right recipe for it. I now have found this amazing woman who makes and sells it at my local market, and it is truly delicious.

Because tempeh is a fermented food, it is considered a much healthier way of eating soya beans than tofu.

Put the spices in a bowl, add the ginger, garlic, oil, lemon juice and yoghurt and mix to combine. Mix in the cauliflower, capsicum, broccoli and tempeh. Cover and marinate for a couple of hours or as long as time permits.

Preheat the oven to 200°C. Line a large baking tray with baking paper.

Spread the marinated tempeh and vegetables on the prepared tray and bake for 30 minutes, until the vegetables are soft. Sprinkle with the basil leaves and toasted cashews and serve with the brown rice.

Serves 4

½ teaspoon sea salt
1 teaspoon ground coriander
1 teaspoon chilli powder
1 teaspoon sweet paprika
1 teaspoon turmeric
1 teaspoon garam masala
1 teaspoon ground cumin
3 cm piece of fresh ginger, peeled and grated
2 garlic cloves, crushed
3 tablespoons olive oil
3 tablespoons lemon juice
130 g (½ cup) Greek-style yoghurt
200 g cauliflower, broken into florets
1 red capsicum, chopped
200 g broccoli, broken into florets
375 g tempeh, cut into thick matchsticks
Thai basil leaves, to serve
50 g toasted unsalted cashews, to serve
steamed brown rice, to serve

dinner

Roast vegetables with sticky vinegar

Often I will just have roast vegetables for dinner. I like to roast a tray of vegetables and then use what I don't eat in a soup or a frittata or on top of a tart. I don't waste time peeling the vegetables as the skin is where the fibre is.

Preheat the oven to 200°C.

Arrange the carrots, shallots, parsnips and garlic on a baking tray and drizzle on the olive oil. Put the pumpkins on another baking tray. Bake for 40–50 minutes, until the vegetables are soft.

Add the tomatoes to the vegetables and drizzle with the vinegar. Return the tray to the oven and bake for 15 minutes more, until the vegetables are soft and sticky.

Serves 4–6

2 bunches of baby carrots, trimmed
500 g French shallots, unpeeled
4 parsnips
1 garlic bulb, broken into cloves, unpeeled
2 tablespoons olive oil
4 small pumpkins
4 heirloom tomatoes, halved
2 tablespoons sherry vinegar

Gazing at a candle flame for 15 minutes before bed or on rising is a wonderful way to balance the pineal and pituitary glands and to calm and align the energy.

Slow-roasted lamb shoulder with rosemary and orange

I don't eat a lot of meat, basically because I prefer vegetables and I love cows. I do, however, sometimes feel I need a boost of iron, so I will cook some red meat. I prefer it to be slow-cooked and to be served with plenty of vegetables. As a rule of thumb, nutrition experts say we only need as much meat as would fit in the palm of our hand. This lamb is so tender that it does not need to be carved, it will simply fall apart.

Preheat the oven to 160°C.

Arrange the carrot, celery, onion, orange and rosemary in a roasting tin and put the lamb on top. Drizzle the olive oil over the lamb, season generously with salt and pepper and pour the wine over the vegetables. Cover with foil and roast for 4 hours. Remove the foil and roast for 1 hour more, until the lamb slips away from the bone when touched with a fork.

Serve the lamb accompanied by the oranges and roast vegetables.

Serves 6

2 carrots, coarsely chopped
3 celery stalks, coarsely chopped
3 red onions, cut into wedges
2 oranges, cut into wedges
4 rosemary sprigs
1 x 1.8 kg organic lamb shoulder
olive oil, for drizzling
sea salt and cracked black pepper
250 ml (1 cup) white wine
roast vegetables of your choice, to serve

Poached chicken with ginger and spring onion sauce

Another ginger-worshipping recipe, this one is my special light dinner I serve to guests. I know the preparation may sound a little dodgy: cooking the chicken for only 20 minutes, then allowing it to cool completely, but trust me, I have cooked this a gazillion times and never had any worries. This method of cooking gives you the most succulent chicken you will ever taste. I love to serve it with lots of steamed Asian greens and baked sweet potato with black sesame and maple.

The sauce is also delicious served over fish or tofu.

Place the chicken, spring onion, star anise, cinnamon, ginger, rice wine and tamari in a large saucepan, cover with water and simmer over low–medium heat for 30 minutes. Cover the pan with a tight-fitting lid, then leave the chicken to poach for 2 hours. (Don't freak out, it will be cooked after this time.)

To make the sauce, combine the ginger, spring onion, 3 tablespoons of warm stock from cooking the chicken, the sesame oil and tamari and mix to combine.

Pour the sauce over the chicken, scatter on the coriander and serve with the steamed greens and brown rice.

Serves 4

1 x 1.6 kg free-range chicken
4 spring onions, chopped
2 star anise
1 cinnamon stick
6 slices of fresh ginger
125 ml (½ cup) Chinese rice wine
2 tablespoons tamari
coriander leaves, to serve
steamed Asian and mustard greens, to serve
steamed brown rice, to serve

Ginger and spring onion sauce
2 tablespoons finely shredded fresh ginger
3 spring onions, thinly sliced
¼ teaspoon sesame oil
2 tablespoons tamari

Both Ayurvedic and Chinese medicine have been using ginger for the past five thousand years to warm, cleanse and stimulate the body. In India and throughout Asia, ginger is added to foods that are cooling to make them more digestible.

Mussels with spicy tomato broth and herbed millet

To make the herbed millet, put the millet into a saucepan, cover with 750 ml (3 cups) of water and bring to the boil. Reduce the heat to low, cover and cook for 25 minutes, until the millet is tender and the liquid has been absorbed. Stir in the chopped herbs, cover and set aside.

Heat the oil in a large saucepan, add the onion and cook, stirring occasionally, over medium heat for 10 minutes. Stir in the garlic and chilli and cook for 1 minute. Add the tomato, orange zest, star anise and wine and bring to the boil. Simmer for 5 minutes, add the mussels and cook for 5 minutes more, until all the shells have opened. Discard any unopened mussels.

Spoon the herbed millet into four serving bowls and top with the mussels and broth. Scatter on the herbs and chilli.

Serves 4

1 tablespoon olive oil
1 red onion, thinly sliced
2 garlic cloves, thinly sliced
1 long red chilli, seeded and sliced
4 tomatoes, chopped
1 teaspoon finely grated orange zest
2 star anise
250 ml (1 cup) white wine
1 kg black mussels, scrubbed and debearded
a handful of chopped flat-leaf parsley, oregano and basil leaves, to serve
1 ancho chilli, finely shredded

Herbed millet
305 g (1½ cups) millet, rinsed
a handful each of flat-leaf parsley, oregano and basil leaves, chopped

Fish baked in salt, pepper and chilli crust

Preheat oven to 180°C.

Rinse the fish and pat dry.

Mix the salt with the egg whites, pink peppercorns, chilli and lemon zest – it should look like wet sand. Spread half the salt over the base of a baking dish large enough to fit the fish. Arrange the fish on top. Fill the cavity of the fish with the herbs. Cover with the remaining salt, pressing down to ensure there are no holes.

Bake the fish for 40 minutes, until a skewer inserted into the centre of the fish comes out hot.

Crack the salt crust with a large spoon and lift it away. To serve, transfer the fish to a large plate and remove the skin.

Serves 4–6

2 large plate-size white fish (bream, snapper), cleaned but not scaled
1.5 kg cooking salt
4 free-range egg whites, lightly beaten
2 tablespoons pink peppercorns, lightly crushed
2 tablespoon finely shredded dried ancho chilli
zest of 1 lemon
a handful of parsley
a handful of oregano

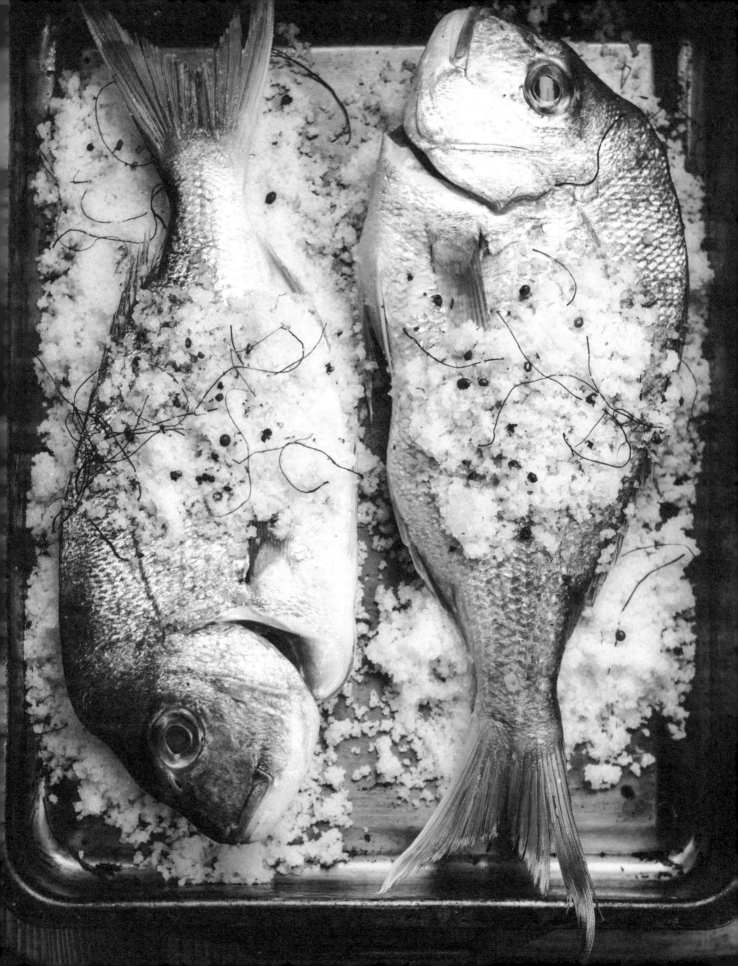

Salmon with charred corn quinoa salsa

Quinoa is the new superfood. It is heating and high in protein, and a great source of energy. You need to rinse it before cooking to wash off the saponin. Cook it only until the tails start to separate; overcooking will make it watery and mushy.

Cook the quinoa in a saucepan of boiling water for 15 minutes, until white tails appear. Rinse under cold water and drain well. Set aside to cool.

Meanwhile, cook the broad beans in a saucepan of boiling water for 5 minutes. Rinse and allow to cool, then peel off the skins.

Heat the barbecue or a large frying pan to hot. Add the corn and capsicum and cook for 10 minutes, until tender and slightly charred on all sides. Allow to cool slightly, then slice the capsicum.

Shave the corn kernels off the cob and place in a bowl, add the quinoa, broad beans, capsicum, kale, tomatoes and pepitas.

Combine the herbs, peppercorns, garlic, salt and olive oil in a mortar and pestle and pound to a coarse paste, then stir into the corn salsa.

To make the dressing, whisk the ingredients together, then pour over the quinoa mixture. Gently stir in the watercress.

Heat the barbecue chargrill plate or a large frying pan to medium–hot and lightly brush with some oil. Add the salmon cutlets and cook for 3 minutes on each side, until cooked to your liking.

Serve the salmon on top of the salsa.

Serves 4

200 g (1 cup) tricolour quinoa, rinsed
150 g broad beans, peeled
2 corn cobs
1 red capsicum
75 g baby kale
200 g cherry tomatoes
2 tablespoons pepitas
a handful of basil leaves
a handful of flat-leaf parsley leaves
1 teaspoon pink peppercorns
1 garlic clove, peeled
pinch of sea salt
3 tablespoons olive oil, plus extra for brushing
2 large handfuls of watercress
4 salmon cutlets

Dressing
1 clove garlic, chopped
1 teaspoon dijon mustard
1 tablespoon verjuice
2 tablespoons olive oil

Preserved lemons

Cut the lemons into quarters lengthways, taking care not to cut all the way through, and stuff the cavity of each lemon with salt.

Put the lemons, bay leaves and peppercorns into a clean 2 litre (8 cup) glass jar, pressing down firmly. Leave unopened on the kitchen bench for 3–4 days.

Press down again on the lemons and pour in the lemon juice, making sure the juice completely covers the lemons. Seal the jar and leave in a cool, dark place for at least 1 month.

Makes 1 x 2 litre (8 cup) jar

1 kg lemons, scrubbed
210 g (⅔ cup) coarse rock salt
2 bay leaves
½ teaspoon black peppercorns
juice of 1 kg lemons

Moroccan chicken with preserved lemon and olives

Preheat the oven to 180°C.

Put the saffron threads into a bowl, add 1 tablespoon of boiling water and allow to stand for 20 minutes.

Cut the chicken into eight pieces, discarding the back bone.

Heat the oil in a large flameproof casserole dish over medium heat, add the chicken, in batches, and cook on all sides until browned. Remove from the dish. Add the onion and cook for 10 minutes, until soft and golden. Stir in the garlic and spices and cook for 2 minutes, until fragrant. Return the chicken to the pan, add the saffron and soaking liquid, the stock and bay leaf and bring to the boil. Cover with a lid and transfer to the oven to bake for 1 hour, until the chicken is tender.

Stir the lemon juice, parsley, preserved lemon and olives into the chicken and simmer, uncovered, on the stovetop for 10 minutes, until the sauce is reduced and thickened slightly. (You may need to remove the chicken pieces to avoid overcooking them.)

Serves 4

½ teaspoon saffron threads
1 x 1.6 kg free-range chicken
2 tablespoons olive oil
2 brown onions, grated
2 garlic cloves, chopped
¼ teaspoon ground ginger
½ teaspoon ground cinnamon
1 teaspoon ground cumin
300 ml chicken stock
1 bay leaf
juice of 1 lemon
2 tablespoons chopped flat-leaf parsley leaves
peel of 1 large preserved lemon, thinly sliced
12 green olives

Beef tagine

The secret of a good tagine is in the spices. Try to ensure that your spices are fresh. The longer you leave the meat in the marinade, the more intense the flavour will be.

Put the steak into a bowl, add the ginger, chilli powder, allspice, turmeric and 1 tablespoon of olive oil, toss to coat. Cover and refrigerate overnight, if time allows. Return to room temperature for 30 minutes before cooking.

Soak the saffron in 2 tablespoons of boiling water for 10 minutes.

Heat the remaining oil in a large heavy-based saucepan over medium–high heat, add the meat, in batches, and cook until browned on all sides. Remove from the pan.

Add the onion to the pan and cook, stirring, over medium heat for 10 minutes, until golden. Return the meat to the pan, add the saffron and its soaking liquid, the cinnamon stick, tomatoes and 400 ml of water and bring to the boil. Reduce the heat, cover and simmer for 40 minutes.

Stir the capsicum, carrot, eggplant, zucchini and almonds into the pan and cook for 30 minutes, until the meat is tender and falling apart.

While the tagine is cooking, put the millet into a saucepan, add 875 ml (3½ cups) of water and bring to the boil. Lower the heat, cover with a tight-fitting lid and cook until all the liquid has been absorbed, about 25 minutes. Fluff the grains with a fork to separate.

Swirl the harissa into the yoghurt.

Sprinkle the chopped coriander over the beef tagine and serve accompanied by the millet and the harissa yoghurt.

Serves 4

500 g organic chuck steak, cut into 4 cm cubes
1 teaspoon ground ginger
½ teaspoon chilli powder
1 teaspoon allspice
1 teaspoon turmeric
2 tablespoons olive oil
pinch of saffron threads
1 red onion, chopped
1 cinnamon stick
400g can chopped tomatoes
1 red capsicum, chopped
2 carrots, cut into thick slices
3 small Japanese eggplants, sliced in
   half lengthways
1 zucchini, cut into thick slices
2 tablespoons whole almonds
420 g (2 cups) millet, rinsed
2 teaspoons harissa
250 ml (1 cup) Greek-style yoghurt
2 tablespoons roughly chopped coriander leaves

treats

Buckwheat and nutmeg baked custard

Buckwheat is a grain – technically it is a grass – that I'm just getting to know. I like to roast it until a nutty brown colour and cook it with milk for brekkie. Buckwheat is a good substitute for those allergic to grains. It is said to help support and strengthen the intestinal tract, making it a great choice for coeliacs.

Preheat the oven to 160°C.

Bring a saucepan of water to a rapid boil, add the buckwheat and cook over high heat for 15 minutes, until the buckwheat is soft. Drain well and cool slightly.

Whisk together the eggs, sugar, milk and nutmeg in a bowl, then add the cooled buckwheat.

Pour the custard and buckwheat mixture into a baking dish, place the dish in a large roasting tin and pour in enough boiling water to come halfway up the sides of the baking dish. Bake for 50 minutes, until the custard is just set. Carefully remove the baking dish from the water bath.

Serve the baked custard with the poached fruit.

Serves 4–6

100 g (½ cup) buckwheat, rinsed
4 free-range eggs
90 g (⅓ cup) coconut sugar
750 ml (3 cups) unhomogenised organic milk
¼ teaspoon freshly grated nutmeg
poached fruit of your choice, to serve

Sweet salty spiced nuts and seeds

Preheat the oven to 160°C. Line a baking tray with baking paper.

Put the nuts, spices, salt, chia and sesame seeds into a bowl, pour over the rice syrup and mix to coat well.

Spread the nut mixture on the baking tray and bake for 20 minutes, until crisp and golden.

Eat immediately or allow to cool before transferring to an airtight container to store for up to 1 week.

Makes 280 g (2 cups)

280 g (2 cups) mixed raw nuts (such as macadamias, pecans, almonds, hazelnuts)
1 teaspoon ground cinnamon
1 teaspoon ground ginger
¼ teaspoon black sea salt
1 tablespoon black chia seeds
2 tablespoons sesame seeds
1 tablespoon brown rice syrup

Slow-cooked pink quinces

Quinces equal windy autumn days for me. They are one of those rare fruits that must be cooked, and the transformation that occurs is really wonderful: their dull white flesh morphs into a stunning pink. At home, I pile them into a big bowl and give them pride of place so that I can admire their fragrant beauty every time I walk past. These quinces are also superb with the Steamed vanilla and green tea custards on page 132.

Put the quinces into a large saucepan, add the ghee, spices, apple juice, lemon juice and 2 litres (8 cups) of water and cook over medium heat for 3 hours, until the quinces turn pink and the flesh is very soft, but not mushy.

Serve with the baked custard.

Serves 4

4 quinces, peeled and halved
2 tablespoons ghee (page 122), melted
1 cinnamon stick
1 bay leaf
2 star anise
1 small dried red chilli
3 cardamom pods, bruised
250 ml (1 cup) unsweetened apple juice
1 tablespoon lemon juice
Buckwheat and nutmeg baked custard
    (page 186), to serve

Gingerbread

In winter, ginger is my go-to spice. The combination of fresh and dried works really well in this moist gingerbread.

Preheat the oven to 170°C. Grease and line a 35 cm x 25 cm baking tin with baking paper.

Melt the butter in a saucepan over low heat. Stir in the sugar, golden syrup, molasses, fresh and ground ginger, cinnamon, cloves and rosewater. Remove from the heat and allow to cool slightly. Add the eggs and mix well.

Sift the flour, baking powder and bicarbonate of soda into a bowl, then mix in the almond meal.

Fold the dry ingredients into the egg mixture, then fold in the chia seeds to make a thin batter.

Pour into the prepared tin and bake for 20–30 minutes, until risen and firm. Be careful not to overcook the gingerbread, as it is better slightly sticky.

Allow the gingerbread to cool in the tin before turning out onto a wire rack. Cut into squares or shapes. Store in an airtight container for up to 1 week.

Serves 8

100 g butter
100 g (½ cup, lightly packed) dark brown sugar
150 g golden syrup
100 g molasses
2 teaspoons finely grated fresh ginger
2 teaspoons ground ginger
1 teaspoon ground cinnamon
¼ teaspoon ground cloves
2 tablespoons rosewater
3 free-range eggs, lightly whisked
100 g (¾ cup) gluten-free plain flour
1 teaspoon gluten-free baking powder
1 teaspoon bicarbonate of soda
255 g (2½ cups) almond meal
2 tablespoons white chia seeds

Cinnamon and chilli cocoa

I add a pinch of cinnamon and cardamom to every warm, milky thing I make in winter, including porridge and hot drinks. I learnt this trick when I first studied Ayurveda and it has remedied my anxious mornings and what could have been sleepless nights.

Combine the cacao, cardamom, cinnamon, chilli, milk and chocolate in a saucepan over medium heat. Cook, stirring several times to stop the chocolate catching on the bottom of the pan, for 15 minutes, until the chocolate has melted. Keep an eye on it: if the heat is too high, it will boil over.

Add the sugar to the pan and stir until it dissolves. Strain.

Serves 4

2 tablespoons cacao powder
6 cardamom pods, bruised
1 cinnamon stick
1 long dried red chilli
1 litre (4 cups) unhomogenised organic milk
   or unsweetened almond milk
100 g dark chocolate, chopped
1 tablespoon coconut sugar

Chocolate, beetroot and raspberry brownie

I could write a whole book on chocolate and the ongoing debate about whether it is good for you. Dark chocolate contains antioxidants, which can be beneficial to your health; however, this doesn't mean I recommend eating it everyday. I see it as a treat and I don't classify treats as something you have at the end of every meal.

Preheat the oven to 180°C. Line the base and sides of a 23 cm square cake tin with a piece of baking paper and allow the paper to extend 5 cm above the sides to make the brownie easy to remove from the tin.

Put the grated beetroot, nut butter, eggs, cacao, rice syrup, bicarbonate of soda, chocolate and dried raspberries into a bowl and mix to combine.

Pour the chocolate mixture into the prepared tin and bake for 40 minutes, until the brownie is still a little gooey when you insert a skewer in the centre.

Remove the brownie from the oven, place on a wire rack and allow to cool in the tin. Remove from tin, then cut into squares

Makes 16

250 g cooked beetroot (about 4 small), grated
250 g (1 cup) super spread or nut butter, at room temperature
2 free-range eggs, lightly whisked
2 tablespoons cacao powder
3 tablespoons brown rice syrup
1 teaspoon bicarbonate of soda
125 g dark chocolate, chopped
100 g dried raspberries

Nut butter is oily and warming, making it ideal for Vata types. Pitta and Kapha doshas should use it in moderation.

Rhubarb and spice quinoa crumble

This great, last-minute winter dessert is always a hit. The quinoa topping can be thrown together in a matter of minutes and it is much lighter than the traditional oat topping.

Preheat the oven to 180°C.

Put the rhubarb, ginger and apple juice into a baking dish and bake for 20–30 minutes, until just soft. Try not to stir the rhubarb during cooking or it will break up.

Spoon the rhubarb and the cooking juices into four ovenproof serving dishes and place on a baking tray.

Tip the quinoa flakes into a bowl, add the coconut sugar, ghee, spices and pepitas and mix well. Pile on top of the stewed rhubarb and bake for 10–15 minutes, until the crumble is crisp and golden.

Serves 4

500 g rhubarb, cut into 5 cm pieces
a thumb-sized piece of fresh ginger, grated
250 ml (1 cup) unsweetened apple juice
95 g (1 cup) quinoa flakes
2 tablespoons coconut sugar
2 tablespoons ghee (page 122), softened
1 teaspoon ground cinnamon
1 teaspoon mixed spice
1 tablespoon pepitas

Fluffy scones

I developed this super-light gluten-free scone recipe for the blog I write for Jamie Oliver. As with all gluten-free baking, these scones are best straight out of the oven.

Preheat the oven to 220°C. Line a baking tray with baking paper.

Put the flours, baking powder, almond meal and salt into a bowl, make a well in the centre and pour in the combined cream and milk. Mix until the dough just comes together.

On a lightly floured surface, pat the dough out to about 4 cm thick. Using a lightly floured 6 cm round cutter, cut scones out of the dough. Place the scones on the prepared tray so that they are touching each other. Lightly brush the tops with the extra milk and bake for 10 minutes, until risen and golden.

Break the scones in half while warm and serve with the jam, stewed rhubarb and whipped cream.

Makes 8

130 g (1 cup) gluten-free plain flour
45 g (¼ cup) white rice flour
2 teaspoons gluten-free baking powder
25 g (¼ cup) almond meal
a good pinch of sea salt
3 tablespoons pure cream
125 ml (½ cup) unhomogenised organic milk,
   plus a little extra for brushing
strawberry jam (100% fruit)
stewed rhubarb, to serve
whipped cream, to serve

Polenta baklava puddings with bay blood oranges

Polenta makes a great dessert. You can choose to spice up the milk and serve it with poached fruit, or add some warming spices to the oranges as I have done here. These puddings are best served warm with Honey pepper yoghurt (page 150).

Lightly grease four 250 ml (1 cup) dariole moulds with ghee or olive oil.

Heat the milk in a saucepan over medium heat until just about to boil. Add the polenta in a fine steady stream and whisk until the polenta starts to thicken. Cook, stirring with a wooden spoon, until the polenta comes away from the side of the pan. Remove from the heat, stir in the maple syrup, cinnamon and nuts and press into the prepared moulds. Allow to stand while you cook the oranges.

Slice 2 of the oranges and juice the 2 remaining oranges. Put the orange slices, juice, bay leaf and cloves into a saucepan and cook over medium heat for 5 minutes, until the sauce is heated through and the orange slices are soft.

Invert the puddings onto serving plates, then spoon the orange slices and sauce around them. Drizzle with the honey and serve.

Serves 4

375 ml (1½ cups) soy milk
35 g (¼ cup) fine polenta (cornmeal)
1 tablespoon pure maple syrup
1 teaspoon ground cinnamon
2 tablespoons chopped almonds
2 tablespoons toasted pine nuts, roughly chopped
2 tablespoons chopped walnuts
4 blood oranges
1 bay leaf
2 whole cloves
2 tablespoons honey, to drizzle

GLOSSARY

adzuki are small, reddish-brown coloured beans, found in Asian food stores or health food stores. Soak them in water overnight before cooking. You can also buy organic adzuki in cans.

arrowroot is a soft, white, gluten-free starchy powder used to thicken sauces. It sometimes appears in gluten-free flour mixes. If you are using it to thicken, you will need to blend it with a little water, as you would cornflour, before stirring it into your dish. Be aware that it doesn't like high temperatures. You will find arrowroot with the flours at your supermarket. Cornflour can be used as a substitute.

bancha tea is made from aromatic green tea twigs. In macrobiotics we make a drink called umeshoban, which we drink when we have a cold. It is a combination of umeboshi plums, shoyu (Japanese soy sauce) or tamari and bancha tea. I also use bancha tea when I have a headache (which isn't often) and serve it to anyone who is suffering when coming off coffee. I really love the taste, so I don't just save it for when I am not well. Like green tea, it contains powerful antioxidants. Find it in Asian food stores.

black sea salt (also known as black lava sea salt) is simply sea salt that has been coloured with activated charcoal. It is said to help detoxify the body and aid digestion.

black vinegar is found in Asian food stores. It has a full, malty, slightly smoky flavour and is made by fermenting glutinous rice with millet. You will need to check the label if you are on a gluten-free diet as some varieties are fermented using wheat protein. Use a mild rice vinegar as a substitute.

brown rice flour is a fantastic gluten-free flour made by grinding unpolished bran. It is a good source of fibre and suitable for cakes, pastries, batters and biscuits.

brown rice syrup is a golden-coloured syrup made from brown rice that has been treated with enzymes to break it down into simple starches and sugars; this mixture is then boiled. It is a good substitute for sugar and considered to be a healthier option.

cacao powder, not to be confused with cocoa, is made from the raw unprocessed cacao bean. Cocoa butter and a sweetener are added to this powder to make chocolate. Cacao powder can be bitter so you will probably need to add a little sweetener. It can be used in baked or raw sweets or drinks.

chamomile are small, daisy-like flowers that are dried to make tea. Chamomile tea is believed to settle the stomach, ease insomnia and anxiety, and relieve constipation. Pregnant and breastfeeding women are not recommended to use it.

chia seeds are small grey or black seeds that take on a mucilaginous quality when added to water. To make a great vegan substitute for an egg, mix 1 tablespoon of chia seeds with 3 tablespoons of water. I use this mixture to lightly set things in place of gelatine, but remember you will still be able to see the seeds. Chia seeds don't have much flavour. They are considered a superfood and are high in protein, fat, fibre and omega-3 fatty acids.

chickpea flour, also known as besan, gram or garbanzo flour, is a great, easy to use gluten-free flour. It is yellow in colour and is often used in Indian cooking to make pakoras or doughs. You can purchase it in health food stores and Asian food stores.

chipotle in Adobo can be found in cans in delicatessens or good food stores. It is a spicy Mexican sauce with whole smoked jalepeños, known as chipotle, in a rich sauce made from chillies, vinegar, herbs and spices. It is great folded through yoghurt, mayonnaise or salsa, or used in marinades. Store any left-over sauce in an airtight container in the fridge for 2 weeks.

chlorophyll (liquid) is considered a superfood. It is incredibly rich in minerals, and helps build and cleanse the blood, detoxify the body, reduce inflammation and fight infection. I like to include a shot in my smoothies and I'll often add it to soups, salad dressings or any dish with leafy greens. Chlorophyll is made from blue-green algae sources, such as spirulina and chlorella. It is considered cooling on the digestive system, so I won't have too much of it in winter unless I warm it.

coconut sugar is a relatively new sugar for me. It has a mild flavour and looks and tastes very similar to brown sugar. I use it because it has a low glycaemic index (35), making it more suitable for diabetics. It is produced from coconut palm blossoms and is considered sustainable. Purchase it from health food stores and the health food section at supermarkets. I always buy organic.

dashi stock is a combination of dried bonito flakes (fermented tuna) and kombu (seaweed). There is a shiitake mushroom variety that is suitable for vegetarians. Dashi is widely used in Japan to flavour soups, dipping sauces, dressings, simmered dishes and stocks. To make your own, soak 1 piece of kombu in 1.25 litres (5 cups) of water overnight, then strain the liquid into a saucepan and bring to a simmer. Add 30 g shaved bonito (katsuobushi), turn off the heat and allow to steep for 5 minutes, then strain. Use the strained stock immediately or refrigerate for up to 4 days or freeze. Alternatively, buy sachets of instant dashi powder from health food stores and the health food section in supermarkets. A lot of commercial dashis contain sugar, so check the packet carefully.

edamame (soya beans) are sold shelled in the freezer department of supermarkets and Asian food stores.

eggs I know everyone knows what eggs are but I just wanted to speak a bit about them here. I do not buy anything but free-range eggs and I don't even think it should be legal to produce anything but. Free-range chickens get to roam around outside, flap their wings and scratch in the dirt – as chickens should. For many years I had my own chooks and they gave me the best eggs I have ever tasted or cooked with. When I can, I buy organic eggs, as they taste most similar to grown-at-home eggs. I encourage you to purchase what you can afford and know that you get what you pay for when it comes to these little darlings.

fish sauce is a dark, amber-coloured liquid that stinks – there is no nice way of putting it – but tastes amazing. Thai and Vietnamese recipes would be lost without it. It has a full-bodied salty flavour and is best combined with lime juice and a little coconut sugar to help balance the salty flavour. Squid brand is my favourite as it has depth of flavour along with saltiness; other brands are way too salty. Fish sauce is made by layering fresh fish (often anchovies) and salt into earthenware tubs, which are then left in the sun for 9 months to 1 year to ferment.

goji berries were once considered the most nutrient-dense food on earth. These small, bright red, dried berries gained popularity about five years ago because of their health-giving properties. They are loaded with vitamin C and iron, are anti-inflammatory, antifungal and antibacterial, and are the highest plant source of protein. I add them to anything where I want a sweet burst and a colour hit. I like to bake them, blend them, pound them, poach them or snack on them. Originally they were grown in the Himalayas and are now widely available and less expensive than they were when first discovered by the western world. They can be found in health food sections of supermarkets or in health food stores.

hulled tahini is a paste of ground, hulled sesame seeds. I like to use organic tahini, and purchase it from a health food store. Store it at room temperature out of direct sunlight as it has a high fat content. It goes really hard if left in the fridge.

kombu is the Japanese word used to describe edible dried kelp/seaweed. Olive green or deep dark green in colour, flat and wide and pretty much what you think of when you picture seaweed, kombu is most often found in its dried form in health food stores or Asian food stores. It keeps for a long period of time stored in an airtight container. It is used to make dashi stock.

lavender sugar is available at fancy delicatessens or you can make your own at home; simply add 1 tablespoon of fresh or 1 teaspoon of dried lavender suitable for cooking to 185 g (1 cup) of coconut sugar and allow to infuse for several weeks before using. Store in an airtight container.

linseeds (flaxseeds) are small, oval brown seeds that are rich in omega-3s, dietary fibre and antioxidants. I add these seeds to pretty much everything in winter as they don't have a lot of taste. I sometimes grind the seeds into a meal and add it to cakes or use it in my seed crackers. They are very rich in oil, so keep them in an airtight container away from direct sunlight to stop them from turning rancid.

maca powder is a creamy, brown-coloured powder. Another superfood, this one has received a lot of publicity in relation to menopause and its ability to balance female hormones. It is also said to be an aphrodisiac. Maca powder is produced from the root of a plant that belongs to the radish family and grows 4100 metres above sea level. It was a staple of the Incas, who used it to give them more energy. Pregnant or lactating women should avoid using maca powder. I add maca powder to drinks, smoothies, cakes, biscuits, seed crackers and batters. Don't confuse it with macadamia meal.

matcha green tea powder is one of my all-time favourite flavours. It is a powerful antioxidant and the Japanese use it to flavour breads, sweets, ice cream, jelly, drinks and many other things. To avoid small dots of green in your drink or dessert, blend matcha with a little liquid to form a smooth paste before adding extra liquid. Matcha can be purchased at Asian food stores; price varies depending on the quality.

milk (unhomogenised) is pasteurised milk that still has the fat or cream on top, like it did when you were a kid. Homogenisation involves pushing milk through very small holes to evenly distribute the fat. Ayurvedic medicine recommends we consume unhomogenised milk, as it is believed to be more digestible. It also advises that milk is always warmed, not served cold. I buy only unhomogenised organic milk.

miso is traditionally made from fermented soya beans, salt and some type of fungus to create a salty paste used to flavour soups and stocks. **Shiro miso**, made from fermented white rice, is a light golden colour and is less salty than darker miso. This is my staple miso in summer, but I still have to use it in moderation as the saltiness makes it very heating. **Genmai miso** is made by fermenting brown rice. I use this in winter. It has a big, more intense salt flavour and is very heating. Miso can be purchased in the Asian section of supermarkets or in Asian food stores. Do not boil miso or you will kill the health-giving enzymes created during the fermentation process.

moong dal are small, oval, golden split beans that are widely used in Indian cooking. They make the best and creamiest dhal. Once you cook with them, they will become a pantry staple. Don't confuse them with green mung beans that have not been split. Moong dal is cooling and is considered very gentle on the digestive system. Remember to soak the split beans before cooking.

nori – paper-thin sheets of dried laver seaweed or a type of edible red algae – is used in sushi rolls and is eaten as a snack on its own or as a condiment that is sprinkled over soups, congee and rice dishes. Considered a good source of minerals, especially iodine, it is protein rich and high in fibre. Store nori in an airtight container; once it is exposed to moisture, it softens quickly.

pickled ginger (undyed) is fresh ginger that has been sliced and pickled in a little rice vinegar and sugar. Often companies add a food colouring to pickled ginger to turn it pink – I try to avoid these brands. Pickled ginger is easy to make at home: just follow the instructions for the Pickled vegetables on page 164.

pomegranate molasses is one of my all-time favourite condiments. It is made by reducing pomegranate juice over high heat to form a thick, sticky, sweet-sour syrup. It is widely used in Middle Eastern cooking and can be found in good delicatessens and health food stores, and in shops that stock Middle Eastern foods. I use pomegranate molasses in dressings, dips and sauces, and drizzle it over salads, fruit, drinks, roasted meats and vegetables.

quinoa flakes are rolled quinoa seeds that look like miniature rolled oats. They are gluten free and make a great substitute for oats.

quinoa flour is a high-protein flour made from ground quinoa seed. It is gluten free and great for batters, cakes and biscuits. It has a strong flavour and I prefer to mix it with another gluten-free flour.

raw honey is the only honey I eat. I never heat it over 40°C because in the Ayurvedic world it is believed that heating honey changes its therapeutic qualities, making it toxic. Raw honey is considered to be a superfood with high levels of vitamins, minerals and antioxidants. Honey is also warming, whereas most other sweeteners are cooling. It is believed to have antibacterial and antifungal properties, so is often mixed with turmeric and applied topically to wounds and sores. It is thought that eating local raw honey is a good way to deal with allergies and hayfever.

ras el hanout is a North African spice mix to which I am addicted. It is a combination of pepper, ginger, cumin, coriander, cardamom, cinnamon, nutmeg, paprika, cloves, turmeric and allspice. Exact recipes are hard to find and, believe me, I have searched widely, so I opt to buy it from good delicatessens. Traditionally used in poultry, meat, game and rice dishes, I am yet to find anything it doesn't go with.

rice flakes are rolled rice grains, another great gluten-free alternative to rolled oats.

spirulina is a type of freshwater blue-green algae that is considered a superfood. It has anti-inflammatory, antioxidant and alkalising properties. It is very high in protein and is recommended for those looking to boost their immune system. It usually comes as a powder, but can also be sold as a liquid or tablets. I use the powder a lot in summer in drinks, dressings, savoury muffins and seed crackers. It is considered cooling, so monitor how much you use in the cooler months if you have a sensitive digestive system.

sticky rice (also known as glutinous rice) is a short-grain rice widely used in Asia. It has a high starch content, which creates the 'stickiness'. If you are toasting and grinding it, it does not need to be soaked but if you are making sticky rice, then you must soak it in cold water overnight. It is then drained and steamed rather than boiled. It is found in Asian supermarkets.

sumac is a pinkish maroon-coloured berry that is ground to form a powder. It is used a lot in Middle Eastern cooking where it is sprinkled over salads or added to marinades and rubs. It is slightly sour and goes really well with chicken, seafood and vegetables. Before lemons were grown, sumac was used as the sour flavour in this part of the world.

super spread is a blended mixture of peanuts, chia seeds, cashews, almonds and brazil nuts, and a delicious alternative to nut butter or tahini. I use it in dressings, raw desserts and baking.

tamari is wheat-free soy sauce made by fermenting soya beans. It is a little thicker than regular soy sauce and is not as salty. Find it in the health food section of supermarkets or in health food stores.

tamarind puree is a murky brown paste sold in the Asian section of supermarkets or in Asian food stores. It has a distinctive sour flavour and is widely used in Asian cooking to balance sweet and salty flavours.

tapioca pearls are small white balls that turn translucent when cooked. They are made from starch extracted from the cassava root, and can be used interchangeably with sago, though they are not the same thing. Tapioca pears are available in supermarkets or Asian food stores.

verjuice is the term given to unfermented grape juice. It has a mild wine-like flavour but is nowhere near as intense as wine and, because it has not been fermented, does not taste alcoholic. Use it as you would lemon juice or a mild vinegar. Look for it in supermarkets and delicatessens. If you can't find it, use lemon juice or sherry vinegar instead.

wakame is a delicious dried seaweed widely used in Japanese cooking. I like to add the dried wakame to soups or rice dishes, or soak it in water until soft and serve it as a salad topped with my favourite dressing. It is a great source of magnesium, calcium and iodine. I buy organic Tasmanian wakame from health food stores.

ABOUT AYURVEDA

I discovered Ayurveda when I was training to be a yoga teacher many moons ago. Its simple, wholistic approach to health and wellbeing really resonated with me – so much so that I went on later to study Ayurveda, and learnt invaluable information about using food as medicine.

'Ayurveda' literally translates as the 'science of life'; it is the traditional healing system of India that has been used for thousands of years to help people live balanced, healthy lives. The main focus of Ayurveda is to promote health, prolong life and eliminate disease. I love the way Ayurveda asks us to use nature to help us understand ourselves. It encourages us to live in harmony with nature and eat with the seasons. According to Ayurveda, we are made up of a combination of five elements – water, fire, earth, air and space. These elements combine in humans to form three 'doshas' or what some people call constitutions — Vata, Pitta and Kapha.

• Vata is a combination of air and space.

• Pitta is a mixture of fire and water.

• In Kaphas, earth and water form a duo.

We are often a combination of two doshas, but when you examine the dosha chart on the following pages, you will usually find that one dosha is dominant.

Some very balanced people can be what is called 'tridoshic' – a combination of all three doshas. A healthy person, according to the Ayurvedic text *Sushrut Samhita*, is he or she 'whose doshas are in balance, appetite is good, all tissues of the body and all natural urges are functioning properly, and whose mind, body and spirit are cheerful.'

To determine your dosha, grab a pen and run through the characteristics on the charts. The column with the most ticks is your predominant dosha; the one with a few less is the other dosha you need to be aware of.

"Leave your drugs in the chemist's pot if you can heal the patient with food." Hippocrates

DOSHA CHART

To establish your dosha, run through this chart from the perspective of yourself as a kid, then go through it again, thinking about how you are today. If you are unsure about your result, re-evaluate it after a month or two. We are usually a combination of one or two doshas.

DOSHA	VATA	PITTA	KAPHA
Mental Activity	Always active	Moderate	Dull, slow
Temperament/ Emotions	Fearful, insecure, indecisive. Unpredictable, anxious, flexible, enthusiastic, vibrant. Sun worshipper, loves the heat. Finds close relationships difficult. Under stress is paranoid, restless, suffers physical ailments and anguish. Happiest in nature. Gets upset but forgets easily. Excellent counsellor or teacher.	Aggressive, intelligent, jealous, determined, quick to anger and hate. Hot, irritable, arrogant, acidic. Organised and enjoys leadership. Competitive, success-oriented, driven, quick-tempered or gets upset and holds emotions in. Likes cool temperatures and foods, irritated by the heat. Under stress becomes gluttonous and promiscuous, has a tendency towards ulcers, insomnia, diarrhoea and weight loss.	Calm, slow, maternal, loving. Loves heat; cold damp weather is frustrating. Gathers and stores material possessions. Prefers to do nothing but is usually very hardworking. Overeats and oversleeps under stress and can become greedy, stubborn, attached or anorexic. Takes a lot to upset, tends to withdraw.
Memory	Quick to learn and forget	Learns quickly	Slow to learn, never forgets
Sleep	Scanty, sleeplessness, difficulty falling asleep, under stress insomniac, sleeps on left side	Little but sound, can suffer from insomnia, sleeps on back	Deep, prolonged, loves to sleep, mostly on stomach
Dreams	Quick, active, fearful, flying	Fiery, war, violent, anger	Watery, snow, romantic
Spending	Spends money quickly	Spends on luxury items	Spends on food
Concentration	Difficult to concentrate	Intense	Methodical
Faith	Changeable, spiritual	Fanatic, faith upon knowledge	Faith based upon love
Relationships with others	Moves from one group of friends to another	Jealous, likes their own way, likes to be centre of attention	Possessive, gets very attached

DOSHA	VATA	PITTA	KAPHA
Frame	Thin, very tall, joints protrude, irregular features	Moderate height, athletic, toned	Thick, strong, compact, wide, big hips, thighs, buttocks and chest
Eyes	Small, dull, dry, brown, sunken, nervous, itchy	Sharp, penetrating, green, hazel, grey, yellow, sensitive to light, sometimes yellowish or bloodshot in sclera	Big, attractive, calm, loving, blue or black
Lips	Dry, cracked, black/brown tinge	Red, inflamed, yellowish	Smooth, oily, pale, whitish
Nails	Dry, brittle, rough, break easily	Pink, soft, tender, flexible	Thick, strong, oily, polished
Hair	Dull, brown, knotted, thin, dry, kinky, brittle	Soft, oily, yellow, blonde, red, straight. Prone to early greying and baldness.	Thick, oily, wavy, dark or blonde, abundant
Tongue	Cracked, tremors	Pink, yellow	White
Teeth	Protruded, big and crooked, gums emaciated	Moderate in size, yellowish, soft gums	Strong white
Speech	Fast, nervous, constant, talkative	Sharp and cutting, penetrating, intense	Slow, monotonous, deep, calm
Skin	Dry, rough, cool, brown, black	Soft, oily, yellowish, fair, red, hot, prone to freckles, rashes and sunburn.	Thick, oily, cool, gleaming, pale, white
Appetite	Variable, scanty	Good, excessive, gets angry when hungry. Under stress craves spicy hot foods and alcohol.	Slow but steady
Thirst	Variable	Excessive	Scanty, sparse
Bowel Movement	Dry, hard, constipated	Soft, oily, loose	Thick, oily, heavy, slow, sluggish
Body Temperature	Cool	Hot	Cool
Taste	Sweet, sour, salty	Sweet, bitter, astringent	Pungent, bitter, astringent
Physical Activity	Very active, hyperactive	Moderate	Lethargic, slow, methodical, sedentary, good endurance and stamina

MENU PLANNERS

It's important that you focus mainly on the dominant dosha when using the menu planners on the following pages, but also pay attention to your other dosha. For example, if you are a combination of Vata and Kapha, you will need to watch how much cool food and drink you consume, especially in winter, as these two doshas are both cold in nature. But if you were a combination of Pitta and Vata, you may have a slightly more robust metabolism, as Pitta is heating in nature and would possibly allow you to eat more uncooked foods. But again, this would depend on the individual – no one diet works for every person.

You will notice I have used some foods from both grounding and warming for Vata people; this is because these are the types of foods this dosha should focus on. I have done the same for Pitta and Kapha.

Once you understand your dosha, you can formulate eating and lifestyle patterns that work for you.

Principles of Ayurveda

- Food needs to be hot (usually cooked).
- Food needs to be tasty and easy to digest.
- Food needs to be eaten in proper amounts, not too much or too little.
- Food needs to be eaten on an empty stomach, after your last meal has been digested and not before.
- Foods need to work together and not contradict one another in their actions.
- Foods need to be eaten in pleasant surroundings with proper equipment for their enjoyment.
- Eating should not be rushed.
- Eating should not be a drawn-out affair either.
- It is best to focus on your food while eating.
- Only eat food which is nourishing to your particular constitution and that suits your mental and emotional temperament.

Charaka

PITTA TYPES

Pitta people are ruled by fire and water, so it is important that they focus on keeping these two elements in balance. Because fire is the dominant element, Pitta people need to be particularly mindful of their diet and lifestyle in the hotter months, when they are most likely to develop an imbalance. They also need to watch the amount of heating, spicy and chilli foods they consume throughout the year since they are naturally drawn to intense flavours, and overindulging in them is not recommended.

Pitta governs metabolism, digestion and energy production in the body. Signs of Pitta imbalance include anything related to heat in the body – skin conditions, ulcers, reflux, indigestion, heartburn and excess sweat. Emotionally, they become short-tempered, controlling and impatient.

Sweet, bitter, astringent and cooling foods are best for balancing Pitta. Most sweet fruits are cooling, as are leafy greens and watery vegetables like cucumber and zucchini. Pitta people can cool down their meals and drinks by adding lemons and limes or a good handful of chopped coriander and mint.

A week's menu for Pitta types

	Mon	Tues	Wed	Thu	Fri	Sat	Sun
Breakfast	Coconut, strawberry and quinoa bircher muesli *(page 25)* + coconut water	Raspberry chia pots with maple coconut tops *(page 34)* + The ultimate green hit *(page 28)*	Coconut, strawberry and quinoa bircher muesli *(page 25)* + Chrysanthemum and licorice tea *(page 136)*	Egg white omelette with asparagus, peas and goat's feta *(page 26)*	Poached stone fruit with bay, vanilla, saffron and star anise *(page 30)* + Blueberry, almond and chia muffin *(page 28)*	Baked ricotta with smoky beans, asparagus and kale *(page 24)*	Vegan coconut, banana and chia pancakes *(page 35}*
Lunch	Chopped salad with herbed chicken *(page 40)*	Almost raw salad *(page 58)*	Fig, rocket and mozzarella salad with sticky pecans *(page 42)*	Prawn rice paper rolls with tamarind sauce *(page 42)*	Coconut and kale dhal *(page 62)*	Minted coconut and chicken larb with crisp witlof *(page 44)*	Fish tacos with cabbage slaw *(page 38)*
Dinner	Zucchini, pea and ricotta fritters with garlic tahini yoghurt *(page 54)*	Fish masala *(page 56)*	Felafel *(page 63)*	Indonesian turmeric chicken *(page 56)*	Poached lemongrass tofu with coconut lime rice *(page 48)* + Steamed greens with nori and spiced almond salt *(page 123)*	Watermelon, feta and mint salad with sumac prawns *(page 52)* + Quinoa tabouleh *(page 52)*	Kitchari *(page 118)*
Treat	Banana, macadamia and chocolate bliss balls *(page 76)*			Coconut tapioca with papaya and lime *(page 66)*		Fig tart with maple yoghurt *(page 67)*	

VATA TYPES

Vata types are ruled by air and space, so they can often appear vague or preoccupied. They are creative types who find it hard to sit still. Wind, cold and too much air travel can have a negative effect on these types, as can too much raw or chilled food and drinks. Vata types should eat regular meals because routine is important for them. Vata can easily become imbalanced in the windier, more unsettled months of spring and autumn. Fans and air conditioners can be very disturbing for someone with a Vata imbalance – best to opt for fresh air wherever possible.

Vata is responsible for movement in the body and governs the nervous system and elimination processes in the body. The seat of Vata is in the mind and the belly, so if Vata is out of balance we often experience anxiety or upset tummies. Signs of Vata imbalance show up in areas related to movement – arthritis, constipation, weight loss and digestive problems. Emotionally, Vata types worry more and are prone to anxiety and insomnia.

Vata influences all other doshas, so when Vata is out of balance we can feel very wobbly and uncertain of our place in the world. Balancing and grounding Vata on a regular basis is recommended.

Sweet, sour, salty, oily, warming foods are best for balancing Vata. Any foods that push down into the earth are very grounding for Vata, so roasted root vegetables are considered to be medicine for these types, as are ghee, dairy and cooked sweet fruits. Vata types will benefit from adding warming spices to their foods, especially in the cooler months.

A week's menu for Vata types

	Mon	Tues	Wed	Thu	Fri	Sat	Sun
Breakfast	Comforting congee *(page 85)*	Grilled figs on honeyed nut butter with spiced nuts *(page 86)* + Ginger tea *(page 144)*	Comforting congee *(page 85)*	Sesame and egg fried rice *(page 88)* + Warm your toes winter chai *(page 145)*	Feta and tomato polenta porridge *(page 145)*	Sweet carrot and ricotta pancakes *(page 90)*	Morning poha *(page 92)*
Lunch	Caramelised onion, kale and sweet potato frittata *(page 109)*	Pumpkin and fennel soup with black quinoa *(page 106)*	Millet and vegetable patties with harissa yoghurt *(page 159)*	Pumpkin and spinach dhal *(page 118)*	Warm beetroot, ricotta and walnut salad *(page 98)*	Nourishing chicken soup *(page 162)*	Nori omelette with miso mushroom broth *(page 166)*
Dinner	Steamed vegetables with miso tahini cream *(page 112)*	Kitchari *(page 118)*	Chicken and egg donburi *(page 113)*	Celeriac and parsnip soup *(page 114)*	Indian vegetable and cashew curry *(page 123)*	Salmon with charred corn quinoa salsa *(page 180)*	Slow-roasted lamb shoulder with rosemary and orange *(page 173)* + Roast vegetables with sticky vinegar *(page 172)*
Treat	Warm spice-infused almond milk *(page 93)*	Pear and pumpkin spiced loaf *(page 136)*		Slow-cooked pink quinces *(page 187)* + Buckwheat and nutmeg baked custard *(page 186)*		Creamed rice with baked baby pears *(page 132)*	

KAPHA TYPES

Kapha types are ruled by the elements of earth and water. They are grounded, reliable folk who have incredible stamina, unless they are out of balance, becoming stuck, inflexible and unmotivated. Because earth is the dominant dosha here, Kapha types like routine and structure. Kapha also governs structure in the body; it rules the bones, muscles, fat and tissues.

Kapha is negatively affected by cold and damp conditions, so the cold, wintery, rainy months can see these types sleeping more than necessary; they can suffer from fluid retention, weight gain and asthma, and sometimes develop diabetes. Emotionally, Kapha imbalance can show up as depression or becoming overly attached to people and situations that no longer serve them. It is important for Kaphas to wake up early and to avoid taking an afternoon nap at these times.

Kaphas often crave sweet foods and drinks, which are not good for them at all because they are cooling. They are drawn to dairy, which is best kept to a minimum as it is grounding in its nature. Oily foods like ghee, nuts and cheese should also be used in moderation. Because of their tendency to cold and dampness, Kapha types need to eat more light, dry and warm foods. Warming spices are particularly beneficial for Kaphas.

A week's menu for Kapha-types

	Mon	Tues	Wed	Thu	Fri	Sat	Sun
Breakfast	Smoked salmon kedgeree *(page 144)* + Ginger tea *(page 144)*	Vegetable miso soup *(page 84)*	Feta and tomato polenta porridge *(page 145)* + Ginger tea *(page 144)* or Flu fighter tea *(page 154)*	Vegetable miso soup *(page 84)*	Sesame and egg fried rice *(page 88)*	Shakshuka *(page 155)*	Sweet carrot and ricotta pancakes *(page 90)*
Lunch	Nourishing chicken soup *(page 162)*	Kitchari *(page 118)*	Speckled quinoa sushi *(page 164)*	Millet and vegetable patties with harissa yoghurt *(page 159)*	Pumpkin and fennel soup with black quinoa *(page 106)*	Nourishing buckwheat risotto *(page 168)*	Pumpkin and spinach dhal *(page 118)*
Dinner	Steamed vegetables with miso tahini cream *(page 112)*	Salmon with charred corn quinoa salsa *(page 180)* + Steamed greens with nori and spiced almond salt *(page 123)*	Celeriac and parsnip soup *(page 114)*	Poached chicken with ginger and spring onion sauce *(page 174)*	Indian vegetable and cashew curry (omit cashews) *(page 123)*	Roast vegetables with sticky vinegar *(page 172)*	Mussels with spicy tomato broth and herbed millet *(page 176)*
Treat	Chamomile and orange blossom poached pears *(page 126)*			Rhubarb and spice quinoa crumble *(page 196)*			Slow-cooked pink quinces *(page 187)* + Cinnamon and chilli cocoa *(page 190)*

ACKNOWLEDGEMENTS

First, I would like to thank **Jo Mackay**, my amazing, patient, kind and truly delightful publisher. It has been a pleasure working with such a calm, eloquent, respectful woman. Thank you for your support and encouragement and belief in this book. Thanks also to the team at Harlequin for putting your faith in me.

Next, I must thank the man who stood beside me through the months up to this book being born. He sat by my side day and night as I said goodbye to my beloved dog, Pridey, just days before we began photography. He drove to Sydney with me and helped me truck home boxes and boxes of props. He whispered words of encouragement when I was certain I couldn't make deadlines. And he anchored this crazy, spinning, cooking banshee when she needed it most. My darling **Kegs**, I don't think I could have pulled this one off without you. I love you to bits and I thank the universe every day that you didn't wait another 11 years to speak to me. Your calmness and kindness remedy my fire-horse flightiness and I am a better person with you walking by my side.

To my incredible team who gave more than I ever could have asked or expected. I am absolutely overwhelmed by how much of your hearts, time and talents you so generously gave to this project. **Kelly Boulton**, your creative genius never ceases to amaze and inspire me. Thank you for the countless hours you surrendered to this project, for your vision and for creating such a beautiful book, as you promised you would. **Ashy**, thank you for letting me borrow your mum for two weeks. You rock! **Jared Fowler**, what can I say? You really are a superstar behind that lens; quiet, focused and so damn efficient. Your images are works of art. Thank you for seeing the simple beauty in the food I put down in front of you and for never uttering one word of complaint. **Scott Foster**, my partner in crime in the kitchen, thank you for the love you put into every dish you cooked for this book, for being my anchoring Kapha influence and for being a damn fine bloke, a fantastic dad and a man whom I love and respect immensely.

To my wonderful editor **Megan Johnston**, thank you for your patience, hard work and for never moaning about the stupidly tight schedule. **Justine Harding**, thank you for coming to the rescue and completing the finishing touches, it is so nice to be working with you again.

I also would like to acknowledge the generosity of a few local Bangalow farmers, **Mike** and **Dan**, who let us invade their farms. Thank you for being so relaxed about the whole thing.

To **Brian Tunks** at Bison Homewares, thanks for your lovely pieces and for always being so happy to ship stuff whenever or wherever I ask.

My **friends** and **family**, who were always happy to come and eat when invited, to test and taste and give feedback. I know it was a big ask; thanks for always saying yes. Thank you too for all the love and comfort you gave me on Pridey's passing, your words and understanding made it easier for me to embrace this project with the passion it deserved.

Kristine Duran-Thiessen, I am and shall remain eternally grateful to you for the kindness you showed me when I needed it most. Thank you for selecting and lending me your gorgeous props, for packing them up and delivering them to my door when I just couldn't face that task. You are an angel.

A huge thank you to my dear friends **the Hayes family**: **Lara**, **Billy**, **Zaliah**, **Finnley**, **Gabe** and **Lexan**. I am so grateful to you for opening your home to me and my team at ridiculous hours of the day, in stupid weather so we could shoot our cover. Thanks for always welcoming us with a smile and your true 'our home is your home' hospitality. **Lara Hayes**, a special thank you to you for reminding me how much I love – er, I am not sure that is the right word – making cookbooks.

I would also like to acknowledge my college **IIN** for being the most inspiring nutrition education institute around. Thanks to **Joshua Rosenthal** for gathering together the best in their fields and for providing sensible, liveable nutritional advice to the world. You are an inspiration.

Thank you to my 'dearest motto' **Sarah Tildesley** and 'horizontal man' **Sam Robinson** for sifting through props shops down the coast with me and Kegs while on holidays. Motto, I am so grateful for the time you spent helping me nut out the bones of the book – what a special treat that was.

A huge thank you to the amazing **Jamie Oliver** for your kind words and continued encouragement and support. I feel so blessed to have worked for you for the past few years and to have seen firsthand the joy cooking and eating good food brings into peoples' lives. Your passionate, respectful, fun and tireless approach to changing the way the western world eats is truly incredible and truly inspirational. The world needs more big-hearted courageous people such as you.

And finally, to my la la bear **Pridey** girl, who sat by my side as I wrote every recipe in this book, towards the end with your head on my lap, asking for nothing but giving me so much. I shall never stop missing sharing my life with you, my sweet blue bear. Working alone was made so much more enjoyable for the past 12 years with you by my side. Thank you for being the most incredible companion, friend, confidante, recipe tester, listener, swimmer, stick chaser, paddock walker, navigator, chicken-drumstick lover, loud drinker, super snorer, best ears ever, more-like-a-person-than-a-dog dog. This one's for you, my princess.

Conversion chart

1 metric tablespoon = 20ml
1 metric teaspoon = 5ml
1 cup = 250ml (8 fl oz)

OVEN TEMPERATURES

°C (Celcius)	°F (Fahrenheit)	Gas Mark
120	250	1
150	300	2
160	325	3
180	350	4
200	400	5
220	450	6
240	500	7

Metric Centimeters (cm) Millimeters (mm)	Inches (in)
2-3 mm	⅛ in
5-6 mm	¼ in
1 cm	½ in
2 cm	¾ in
2.5 cm	1 in
5 cm	2 in
6 cm	2 ½ in
8 cm	3 in
10 cm	4 in
13 cm	5 in
15 cm	6 in
18 cm	7 in
20 cm	8 in
23 cm	9 in
25 cm	10 in
28 cm	11 in
30 cm	12 in

DRY AND LIQUID MEASURES

Metric (Grams)	Imperial (Ounces / Pounds)	Metric (Millilitres)	Imperial (Fluid ounces)
30 g	1 oz	30 ml	1 fl oz
60 g	2 oz	60 ml	2 fl oz
90 g	3 oz	90 ml	3 fl oz
125 g	4 oz	125 ml	4 fl oz
150 g	5 oz	150 ml	5 fl oz
180 g	6 oz	180 ml	6 fl oz
200 g	7 oz	200 ml	7 fl oz
250 g	8 oz	250 ml	8 fl oz
280 g	9 oz	280 ml	9 fl oz
310 g	10 oz	310 ml	10 fl oz
340 g	11 oz	340 ml	11 fl oz
375 g	12 oz	375 ml	12 fl oz
500 g	16 oz/ 1lb	500 ml	16 fl oz
1 kg	32 oz/ 2lb	1 litre	32 fl oz

Index

First published October 2014
First Australian Paperback Edition 2014
ISBN 9781743569016

Beautiful Food
© Jody Vassallo 2014

Published by
Harlequin Mira
An imprint of Harlequin Enterprises (Australia) Pty Ltd.
Level 4, 132 Arthur Street
NORTH SYDNEY NSW 2060
AUSTRALIA

Edited by Megan Johnston
Designed and art directed by Kelly Boulton
Photographed by Jared Fowler
Food prepared for photography by Scott Foster
Food styling by Jody Vassallo
Recipe testing by Kristen Ingemar
Colour reproduction by Graphic Print Group, SA
Printed and bound in Singapore by C.O.S. Printers